Disclosure

AF885642

If you have any suggestions or corrections please submit them at https://purpleteamfieldmanual.com/contact

Table of Contents

POST

A Power-On Self-Test (POST) is a diagnostic testing process executed by a computer's Basic Input/Output System (BIOS) immediately after the device is powered on. The primary purpose of POST is to ensure that all required hardware components are present and functioning correctly before the boot process continues. POST checks key components such as the Central Processing Unit (CPU), Random Access Memory (RAM), disk drives (HDD/SSD), and peripheral devices like keyboards and mice.

The results of the POST are communicated through various mechanisms. They may be displayed on a screen or panel, output as audio beep codes, or indicated through LED error codes. Each manufacturer has unique beep codes or POST codes, with specific patterns corresponding to different hardware issues.

Critical errors detected during POST usually halt the boot process, preventing the computer from starting. However, some non-critical errors, such as a missing keyboard or mouse, may allow the system to continue booting with warnings. By ensuring that essential components are operational, POST helps maintain system stability and functionality from the moment the device is powered on.

MBR

The Master Boot Record (MBR) is a critical 512-byte section of a disk that contains essential information for the boot process. It comprises three primary components: the bootloader (446 bytes), the partition table (64 bytes), and the magic number (2 bytes). After completing the Power-On Self-Test (POST), the BIOS looks for the MBR to initiate the boot process.

The typical order of operation involves the BIOS searching for bootable media such as CDs or disk drives. This search order is user-customizable via the BIOS settings. If no such media is found, the BIOS loads the program located on the first sector of the primary disk bus at address 0x7C00 into memory. This sector contains the MBR.

The MBR's 446 bytes of executable code, commonly referred to as the "stage 1" bootloader, are responsible for initiating the boot process. The primary function of this first stage is to locate the main bootloader on the disk, often referred to as the "stage 2" bootloader. Once located, the stage 2 bootloader executes and loads the available kernels and operating systems that are bootable.

The partition table within the MBR holds information about the disk's partitions, including their size, type, and location. This information is crucial for the bootloader to correctly identify and access the partitions where operating systems or other bootable software are installed.

Additionally, the MBR includes a 2-byte magic number, which is a signature used to validate the integrity of the MBR. If this magic number is incorrect, it indicates that the MBR may be corrupted, preventing the system from booting properly.

The MBR scheme has some limitations, such as supporting only up to four primary partitions and disks of up to 2TB in size. For larger disks and more flexible partitioning, the GUID Partition Table (GPT) is often used as a modern alternative to the MBR.

GPT

The GUID Partition Table (GPT) is a modern partitioning scheme that is part of the Unified Extensible Firmware Interface (UEFI) standard, designed to overcome the limitations of the traditional Master Boot Record (MBR) partitioning scheme. Unlike MBR, GPT supports larger disks and a greater number of partitions, making it suitable for contemporary storage requirements.

GPT can handle disks larger than 2TB, which is the maximum supported by MBR. This makes GPT suitable for use with modern large-capacity storage devices. Additionally, GPT allows for a virtually unlimited number of partitions; however, the default configuration typically allows for up to 128 partitions without requiring additional setup.

One of the key features of GPT is its use of primary and backup partition tables, providing redundancy and improving the reliability of the partitioning information. The primary GPT header is located at the beginning of the disk, while the backup GPT header is located at the end of the disk. Each partition entry in GPT includes a globally unique identifier (GUID), ensuring that each partition can be uniquely identified across all systems.

GPT also uses CRC32 checksums to verify the integrity of the partition table and headers. This helps detect and correct errors, enhancing the reliability of the disk. Additionally, a protective MBR is included at the beginning of the disk to prevent legacy MBR-based disk utilities from misinterpreting the GPT disk and potentially overwriting it. The protective MBR contains a single partition that spans the entire disk, indicating that the disk is in use.

GPT supports a variety of partition types and attributes. Each partition entry includes a partition type GUID, a unique identifier for the partition, and attributes that define its properties and behaviors, such as whether it is bootable. Furthermore, GPT is an integral part of the UEFI standard, which replaces the older BIOS firmware interface. UEFI firmware uses GPT to manage and boot from disks, providing a more flexible and powerful boot environment.

Linux boot process

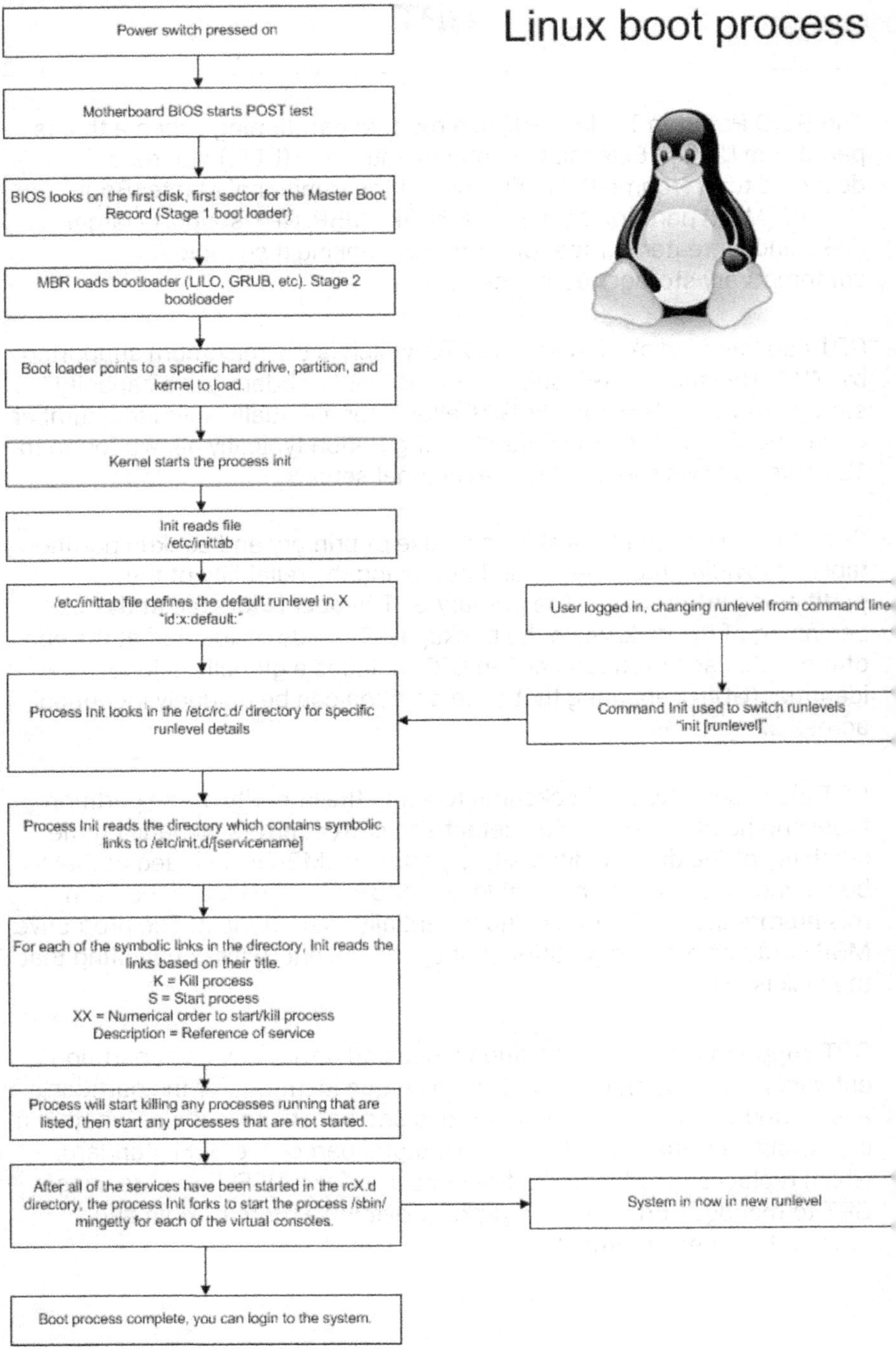

Bootloader

What is it?

A bootloader, also referred to as a bootstrap load or boot program, is an essential part of the boot process that loads into working memory directly after POST

BIOS Boot Loader

The BIOS boots by reading the first sector on a hard disk and executing it; this boot sector, also known as the Master Boot Record (MBR), in turn locates and runs additional code. The BIOS system is very limiting because of space constraints and because BIOS runs 16-bit code, whereas modern computers use 32-bit or 64-bit CPUs. This necessitated the development of more advanced boot systems such as UEFI.

BIOS

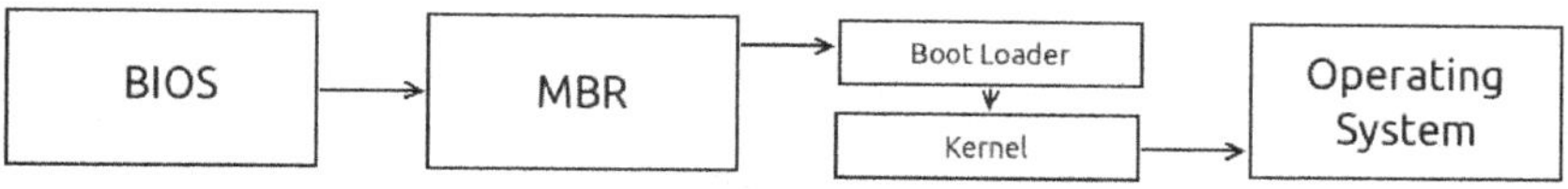

EFI Boot Loader

EFI (or UEFI, which is just EFI 2.x) boots by loading EFI program files (with .efi filename extensions) from a partition on the hard disk, known as the EFI System Partition (ESP). These EFI boot loader programs can take advantage of EFI boot services for tasks such as reading files from the hard disk. UEFI offers a more flexible and powerful boot environment, supporting larger disks and more complex boot processes.

UEFI

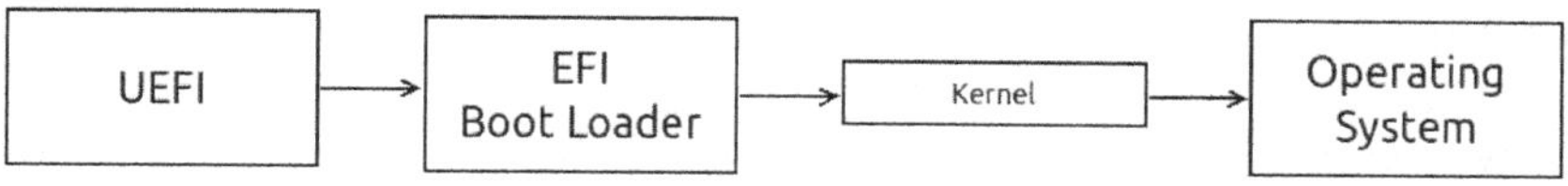

Grub

Overview

GNU GRUB is a multiboot boot loader. It was derived from GRUB, the GRand Unified Bootloader, which was originally designed and implemented by Erich Stefan Boleyn. GRUB 2 has replaced what was formerly known as GRUB (i.e., version 0.9x), which has, in turn, become GRUB Legacy. Enhancements to GRUB are still being made, but the current released versions are quite usable for normal operation.

GRUB 2 Features:

- Modular design, allowing for the addition of modules to extend functionality.
- Support for multiple operating systems and filesystems.
- Customizable boot menu with themes and graphics.

Example Configuration (grub.cfg):

```
menuentry 'Ubuntu' {
    set root=(hd0,1)
    linux /vmlinuz root=/dev/sda1 ro
    initrd /initrd.img
}
```

Menu Commands

The following commands are applicable to GRUB (GRand Unified Bootloader) configurations, providing essential functionalities for managing boot entries and bootloader behavior. These commands allow users to set default boot entries, manage boot sequences, and customize the GRUB menu interface.

<table>
<tr><th>Command</th><th>Result</th><th>Applicability</th></tr>
<tr><td>default <num></td><td>Sets the default boot entry to the entry number num. Numbering starts from 0, and entry number 0 is the default if not specified.</td><td rowspan="2">GRUB Legacy, GRUB 2</td></tr>
<tr><td>fallback <num></td><td>Enters unattended boot mode: if the default boot entry has errors, it immediately starts over using the num entry.</td></tr>
<tr><td>hiddenmenu</td><td>Hides the menu from display. The default entry will be booted after the timeout expires. Press ESC to display the menu.</td><td>GRUB Legacy</td></tr>
<tr><td>timeout <sec></td><td>Sets a timeout in sec seconds before automatically booting the default entry.</td><td>GRUB Legacy, GRUB 2</td></tr>
<tr><td>title <name></td><td>Starts a new boot entry and sets its name to the rest of the line starting with the first non-space character.</td><td>GRUB Legacy</td></tr>
</table>

Boot and Kernel Commands

This table includes commands related to booting the operating system and loading different types of kernels and boot loaders. These commands are crucial for starting the system, switching between different operating systems, and loading necessary components for the boot process.

Command	Description
boot	Start up your operating system
chainloader	Chain-load another boot loader
initrd	Load a Linux initrd
initrd16	Load a Linux initrd (16-bit mode)
linux	Load a Linux kernel
linux16	Load a Linux kernel (16-bit mode)
multiboot	Load multiboot compliant kernel
xen_hypervisor	Load Xen hypervisor binary (only on AArch64)
xen_module	Load Xen modules for Xen hypervisor (only on AArch64)

Configuration and Environment Commands

This table outlines commands used to manage configuration files and environment variables within GRUB. These commands help set and retrieve configuration settings, load and save environment variables, and manage the boot configuration dynamically.

Command	Description
configfile	Load a configuration file
export	Export an environment variable
list_env	List variables in environment block
load_env	Load variables from environment block
save_env	Save variables to environment block
set	Set an environment variable
unset	Unset an environment variable
source	Read a configuration file in the same context

File System and Device Commands

This table contains commands for interacting with the file system and devices. Commands in this category allow users to manage disk mappings, load device trees, and work with filesystem images, providing essential tools for device and disk management.

Command	Description
blocklist	Print a block list
cryptomount	Mount a crypto device
devicetree	Load a device tree blob
drivemap	Map a drive to another
loopback	Make a device from a filesystem image
nativedisk	Switch to native disk drivers
parttool	Modify partition table entries
probe	Retrieve device info
search	Search devices by file, label, or UUID
videoinfo	List available video modes

Security and Authentication Commands

This table lists commands related to security and user authentication within GRUB. These commands help set passwords, manage trusted keys, and verify user identities, ensuring secure access to the boot loader and the system.

Command	Description
authenticate	Check whether user is in user list
password	Set a clear-text password
password_pbkdf2	Set a hashed password
trust	Add public key to list of trusted keys
distrust	Remove a pubkey from trusted keys
verify_detached	Verify detached digital signature

Memory and CPU Commands

This table includes commands for checking and managing memory and CPU features. These commands help identify and manage memory regions, check CPU capabilities, and interact with specific CPU registers, aiding in hardware diagnostics and optimizations.

Command	Description
badram	Filter out bad regions of RAM
cutmem	Remove memory regions
cpuid	Check for CPU features
rdmsr	Read values from model-specific registers
wrmsr	Write values to model-specific registers
smbios	Retrieve SMBIOS information

Filesystem and Disk Commands

This table provides commands for loading and managing modules related to the filesystem and disk operations. These commands are used to list and load font files, insert and remove modules, and handle multiboot kernel modules, facilitating filesystem and disk management.

Command	Description
insmod	Insert a module
lsfonts	List loaded fonts
loadfont	Load font files
lsmod	Show loaded modules
module	Load module for multiboot kernel
rmmod	Remove a module

Checksum and Hash Commands

This table outlines commands for computing and verifying various checksums and hashes. These commands are important for data integrity checks, allowing users to verify the correctness of files and configurations.

Command	Description
crc	Compute or check CRC32 checksums
hashsum	Compute or check hash checksum
md5sum	Compute or check MD5 hash
sha1sum	Compute or check SHA1 hash
sha256sum	Compute or check SHA256 hash
sha512sum	Compute or check SHA512 hash

Miscellaneous Commands

This table lists a variety of commands that do not fit into the other categories but are nonetheless important for specific functions. These include commands for ACPI table management, CMOS operations, playing sounds, and managing video modes, among others, providing additional functionality within the GRUB environment.

Command	Description
acpi	Load ACPI tables
background_color	Set background color for active terminal
background_image	Load background image for active terminal
cmosclean	Clear bit in CMOS
cmosdump	Dump CMOS contents
cmostest	Test bit in CMOS
gettext	Translate a string
gptsync	Fill an MBR based on GPT entries
halt	Shut down your computer
keystatus	Check key modifier status
normal	Enter normal mode
normal_exit	Exit from normal mode
play	Play a tune
reboot	Reboot your computer
regexp	Test if regular expression matches string
sendkey	Emulate keystrokes
date	Display or set current date and time

BURG

BURG stands for Brand-new Universal loadeR from GRUB. It's based on GRUB and adds features like a new object format and a configurable menu system. BURG aims to provide a more visually appealing boot menu with themes and graphical interfaces.

BURG Features:

- Enhanced user interface with themes and icons.
- Customizable menus with various options.
- Compatibility with GRUB's configuration and commands.

Example Configuration (burg.cfg):

```
menuentry 'Ubuntu' {
    set root=(hd0,1)
    linux /vmlinuz root=/dev/sda1 ro
    initrd /initrd.img
}
```

Install

```
sudo add-apt-repository ppa:danielrichter2007/grub-customizer -y &&
sudo apt-get update && sudo apt-get install grub-customizer
```

Customize

```
sudo burg-emu  ### Then press f2 and use arrow keys to select theme
```

Syslinux

SYSLINUX is a boot loader for the Linux operating system that runs on an MS-DOS/Windows FAT filesystem. It is intended to simplify the first-time installation of Linux and to facilitate the creation of rescue and other special-purpose boot disks.

SYSLINUX Features:

- Simple installation and configuration.
- Variants like ISOLINUX for booting from ISO 9660 filesystems and PXELINUX for network booting using PXE.
- Ideal for creating bootable USB drives and rescue disks.

Example Configuration (syslinux.cfg):

```
DEFAULT linux
LABEL linux
    KERNEL vmlinuz
    APPEND initrd=initrd.img root=/dev/sda1 ro
```

Menu Commands

This table provides a comprehensive list of Syslinux menu commands along with their descriptions. Syslinux is a lightweight bootloader for Linux, used to boot operating systems from various media. The commands allow users to manage boot entries, modify input, and display system information during the boot process.

Command	Description
[Enter]	Boots the specified command. Typically used to select and execute the chosen boot entry.
[BackSpace]	Erases one character back. Useful for correcting typing errors in commands.
[Ctrl-U]	Erases the entire command line. Allows users to quickly clear the current input.
[Ctrl-V]	Displays the current Syslinux version. Useful for verifying the version being used.
[Ctrl-W]	Erases one word back. Helps in quickly removing incorrect or unwanted words from the command line.
[Ctrl-X]	Forces text mode. Useful for switching to text mode if there are graphical boot issues.
[Tab]	Lists matching labels. Helps in finding and selecting available boot entries.
[F1]..[F12]	Displays "help" screens if configured. Function keys provide access to additional help screens.
[Ctrl-F][digit]	Equivalent to F1..F9. Provides alternative access to function keys F1 through F9.
[Ctrl-F][0]	Equivalent to F10. An alternative key combination for pressing F10.
[Ctrl-F][A]	Equivalent to F10. Another alternative for pressing F10.
[Ctrl-F][B]	Equivalent to F11. Alternative key combination for pressing F11.
[Ctrl-F][C]	Equivalent to F12. Alternative key combination for pressing F12.
[Ctrl-C]	Interrupts the boot in progress. Useful for stopping the boot process if necessary.
[Esc]	Interrupts the boot in progress. Similar to Ctrl-C, allows users to halt the boot process.
[Ctrl-N]	Displays network info (only in PXELINUX versions 3.50-4.xx). Provides network-related information.

LILO

LILO (LInux LOader) is a bootloader that was created for Linux. LILO was the default bootloader used for most desktop and server distributions for many years. For EFI-based hardware, the ELILO boot loader was developed. LILO ended development in 2015; however, it can still be found on embedded devices.

LILO Features:

- Simple and straightforward configuration.
- Support for various hardware platforms and filesystems.
- Direct booting of Linux kernels without additional stages.

Example Configuration (lilo.conf):

```
boot=/dev/sda
map=/boot/map
install=/boot/boot.b
prompt
timeout=50
image=/boot/vmlinuz
    label=linux
    read-only
    root=/dev/sda1
```

ELILO

ELILO is a bootloader specifically developed for EFI-based systems. It supports the EFI boot process and is used to load Linux kernels on systems with UEFI firmware.

ELILO Features:

- EFI compatibility, enabling it to boot on modern hardware.
- Simple configuration similar to LILO.
- Support for loading initrd images and passing kernel parameters.

Example Configuration (elilo.conf):

```
default=linux
image=vmlinuz
    label=linux
    read-only
    initrd=initrd.img
    append="root=/dev/sda1 ro"
```

Kernel

Overview

The Linux kernel is a set of software components that are called modules. Modules work together as a single system to enable daemons and applications to run on the operating system in an efficient manner. Modules control hardware devices and software components. Not all modules in the kernel are loaded at all times, some are dynamically loaded when needed other modules are static.

When the system is booted the kernel is loaded into memory with all static modules. The dynamic modules are loaded into memory when required. A Linux kernel that is comprised of only static modules is referred to as a monolithic kernel, monolithic kernels are generally larger in size and include all necessary components. Monolithic kernels can be less efficient as they require larger amounts of physical memory. A kernel that is comprised of static and dynamic modules is referred to as modular kernel, modular kernels are made up of critical components and loads dynamic modules into memory as needed.

The Linux kernel is a free and open-source, monolithic, modular, multitasking, Unix-like operating system kernel. It was conceived and created in 1991 by Linus Torvalds for his i386-based PC, and it was soon adopted as the kernel for the GNU operating system, which was created as a free replacement for UNIX.

Kernel files are stored in the /boot, /proc, and /lib/modules directories

Kernel Versions

Kernel Version	Name	Kernel Version	Name
1.2.0	Linux '95	2.6.28	Killer Bat of Doom
1.3.51	Greased Weasel	2.6.29	Temporary Tasmanian Devil
2.2.1	Brown Paper Bag	2.6.30	Vindictive Armadillo
2.4.15	Greased Turkey	2.6.31 - 2.6.32	Man-Eating Seals of Antiquity
2.6.2 - 2.6.4	Feisty Dunnart	2.6.33 - 2.6.34	Sheep on Meth
2.6.5 - 2.6.9	Zonked Quokka	2.6.35	Yokohama
2.6.10 - 2.6.13	Woozy Numbat	2.6.36 - 2.6.39	Flesh-Eating Bats with Fangs
2.6.14	Affluent Albatross	3	Sneaky Weasel
2.6.15 - 2.6.16	Sliding Snow Leopard	3.1	Divemaster Edition
2.6.17	Lordi Rules	3.2 - 3.5	Saber-toothed Squirrel
2.6.18 - 2.6.19	Avast! A bilge rat!	3.6 - 3.7	Terrified Chipmunk
2.6.20	Homicidal Dwarf Hamster	3.8 - 3.10	Unicycling Gorilla
2.6.21	Nocturnal Monster Puppy	3.11	Linux for Workgroups
2.6.22	Holy Dancing Manatees, Batman!	3.12	Suicidal Squirrel
2.6.23	Pink Farting Weasel	3.13	One Giant Leap for Frogkind
2.6.24	Arr Matey! A Hairy Bilge Rat!	3.14	Shuffling Zombie Juror
2.6.25	Funky Weasel is Jiggy wit it	3.18	Diseased Newt
2.6.26 - 2.6.27	Rotary Wombat	4	Hurr durr I'ma sheep

Kernel Version	Name	Kernel Version.	Name
4.1.1	Series 4800	5.12	Frozen Wasteland
4.3	Blurry Fish Butt	5.13	Opossums on Parade
4.6	Charred Weasel	5.14	Trick or Treat
4.7	Psychotic Stoned Sheep	5.15	Superb Owl
4.9	Roaring Lionus	5.16	
4.1	Fearless Coyote	5.17	
4.17	Merciless Moray	5.18	
4.19	"People's Front"	5.19	
4.20 - 5.0	Shy Crocodile	6.0	Hurr durr I'm a ninja sloth
5.2	Bobtail Squid	6.1	
5.4	Kleptomaniac Octopus	6.2	
5.5		6.3	
5.6		6.4	
5.7		6.5	
5.8		6.6	
5.9		6.7	one of the largest kernel releases we've ever had
5.1	Dare mighty things	6.8	
5.11	Valentine's Day Edition	6.9	

Kernel Directories

/boot

The /boot file system is created at system installation, and its purpose is to store kernel-related information, including the current working kernel and associated files. This file system also stores any updated or modified kernel data. Key files and directories within /boot include: vmlinuz-*, the compressed Linux kernel image; initrd.img-* or initramfs-*, initial RAM disk images used to bootstrap the system; config-*, configuration files used for building the kernel; System.map-*, the symbol table for the kernel; and the grub/ directory, which contains GRUB bootloader configuration files.

/proc

The /proc is a virtual file system, and its contents are created in memory at system boot and destroyed when the system powers down. This file system provides an interface to kernel data structures, presenting information about the system and processes in a hierarchical, file-like structure. It contains several files and sub-directories that provide real-time system information. Some key files and sub-directories include: cpuinfo, which contains information about the CPU such as model, speed, and number of cores; meminfo, which provides detailed information about the system's memory usage; and uptime, which displays the system uptime and idle time. The pid/ sub-directories, named with numerical process IDs (PIDs), contain information about specific processes, such as pid/cmdline, which shows the command line of the process; pid/status, which provides process status information; and pid/fd/, a directory containing the file descriptors opened by the process. These directories and files within /proc are instrumental for system monitoring, debugging, and performance tuning, as they provide a dynamic view of the system's state. An example of configuration files are /proc/cpuinfo and /proc/meminfo

```
lfm@LFM:~$ cat /proc/cpuinfo
processor       : 0
vendor_id       : GenuineIntel
cpu family      : 6
model           : 158
model name      : Intel(R) Core(TM) i9-9880H CPU @ 2.30GHz
```

```
lfm@LFM:~$ cat /proc/meminfo
MemTotal:        4002244 kB
MemFree:         1387184 kB
MemAvailable:    2036316 kB
Buffers:           66028 kB
Cached:           743924 kB
```

/lib/modules

The /lib/modules directory holds information about kernel modules. If there are multiple kernels installed on the system, each will have its own sub-directory within /lib/modules. These sub-directories are named after the respective kernel versions and contain module files (*.ko), configuration files, and dependencies necessary for the proper functioning of the kernel modules.

```
lfm@LFM:~$ ll /lib/modules
total 36
drwxr-xr-x   9 root root 4096 Oct 20  2020 ./
drwxr-xr-x 130 root root 4096 Oct 18  2020 ../
drwxr-xr-x   2 root root 4096 Jul 22  2020 5.4.0-26-generic/
drwxr-xr-x   2 root root 4096 Jul 23  2020 5.4.0-33-generic/
drwxr-xr-x   2 root root 4096 Sep  2  2020 5.4.0-37-generic/
drwxr-xr-x   2 root root 4096 Oct 19  2020 5.4.0-42-generic/
drwxr-xr-x   6 root root 4096 Sep  1  2020 5.4.0-45-generic/
drwxr-xr-x   6 root root 4096 Oct 18  2020 5.4.0-51-generic/
drwxr-xr-x   6 root root 4096 Oct 20  2020 5.4.0-52-generic/
lfm@LFM:~$ ll /lib/modules/5.4.0-26-generic/
total 1132
drwxr-xr-x 2 root root   4096 Jul 22  2020 ./
drwxr-xr-x 9 root root   4096 Oct 20  2020 ../
-rw-r--r-- 1 root root 144474 Jul 22  2020 modules.alias
-rw-r--r-- 1 root root 154385 Jul 22  2020 modules.alias.bin
-rw-r--r-- 1 root root  24985 Jul 22  2020 modules.builtin.alias.bin
-rw-r--r-- 1 root root  10257 Jul 22  2020 modules.builtin.bin
-rw-r--r-- 1 root root  84421 Jul 22  2020 modules.dep
-rw-r--r-- 1 root root 122790 Jul 22  2020 modules.dep.bin
-rw-r--r-- 1 root root    268 Jul 22  2020 modules.devname
-rw-r--r-- 1 root root    457 Jul 22  2020 modules.softdep
-rw-r--r-- 1 root root 267670 Jul 22  2020 modules.symbols
-rw-r--r-- 1 root root 316658 Jul 22  2020 modules.symbols.bin
```

The command lsmod will show the modules that are currently loaded into the kernel. It also provides information about the size of each module, the number of instances currently in use, and which modules are using them. However, it does not specify which processes are using the modules.

```
lfm@LFM:/lib/modules/5.4.0-26-generic$ lsmod
Module                  Size  Used by
xt_conntrack           16384  1
xt_MASQUERADE          20480  1
nf_conntrack_netlink    45056  0
nfnetlink              16384  2 nf_conntrack_netlink
xfrm_user              36864  1
xfrm_algo              16384  1 xfrm_user
xt_addrtype            16384  2
iptable_filter         16384  1
iptable_nat            16384  1
nf_nat                 40960  2 iptable_nat,xt_MASQUERADE
```

SELinux

Security-Enhanced Linux (SELinux) is a Linux kernel security module that provides a mechanism for supporting access control security policies, including mandatory access controls (MAC). SELinux is a set of kernel modifications and user-space tools that have been added to various Linux distributions to enhance security by enforcing these policies.

SELinux operates on the principle of least privilege, which means it restricts the access of processes and users to the minimum necessary to perform their tasks. This minimizes the potential damage from vulnerabilities or misconfigurations. SELinux is particularly useful in enhancing the security of a Linux system by controlling access to files, processes, and network resources.

SELinux States

SELinux can operate in three different states, each affecting how it enforces security policies:

State	Description	Practical Significance
enforcing	SELinux security policy is enforced	SELinux denies access and logs actions that violate policy
permissive	SELinux prints warnings instead of enforcing	SELinux does not deny access but logs actions that violate policy; useful for troubleshooting and policy development
disabled	No SELinux policy is loaded	SELinux is not active; the system operates without SELinux protection

Enable/Disable/Status

These commands allow you to check the status of SELinux, enable or disable it temporarily, or configure it to be enabled or disabled permanently.

Action	Command	Description
Check status (detailed)	sestatus	Display detailed status of SELinux
Check status (brief)	getenforce	Display current mode of SELinux (enforcing/permissive/disabled)
Enable (temporarily)	setenforce 1	Enable SELinux temporarily until reboot
Disable (temporarily)	setenforce 0	Disable SELinux temporarily (permissive mode)
Enable/Disable (permanent)	Edit /etc/selinux/config	Change SELINUX= to permissive, enforcing, or disabled for permanent change after reboot

Booleans

SELinux booleans are variables that can modify the behavior of SELinux policies without requiring a policy rebuild. Examples include `httpd_enable_homedirs` for allowing HTTPD access to user home directories.

Action	Command	Description
List all booleans	getsebool -a	List all SELinux booleans
List specific booleans	getsebool -a | grep PATTERN	List specific booleans matching a pattern
Set boolean (until reboot)	setsebool <boolean var> <0/1>	Set the value of a boolean until reboot
Set boolean permanently	setsebool -P <boolean var> <0/1>	Set the value of a boolean permanently

Package Managers

Package managers are essential tools for managing software on Linux systems. They help users install, update, remove, and manage software packages efficiently. Different Linux distributions use different package managers. Here are some of the most common ones:

APT - Debian-based Systems

Advanced Package Tool (APT) is used in Debian, Ubuntu, and other Debian-based distributions. It simplifies the process of managing software packages.

Command	Description
sudo apt install <package_name>	Install a package
sudo apt update	Update package list
sudo apt upgrade	Upgrade all packages
sudo apt remove <package_name>	Remove a package
apt search <package_name>	Search for a package
sudo apt-mark hold <package_name>	Prevent a package from being upgraded (Pinning Versions)
apt-get -f install	Fix broken dependencies
sudo add-apt-repository ppa:<ppa_name>	Add a Personal Package Archive (PPA)
sudo apt update	Update package list after adding a PPA

Adding a Repository

To add a custom repository to APT, you need to add its details to a file in the `/etc/apt/sources.list.d/` directory.

```
echo "deb http://example.com/repository distribution component" |
sudo tee /etc/apt/sources.list.d/example.list
sudo apt update
```

DNF (Dandified YUM) and YUM - Red Hat-based Systems

DNF is the next-generation version of YUM and is used in Fedora, CentOS, and RHEL.

Command	Description
sudo dnf install <package_name>	Install a package with DNF
sudo dnf check-update	Update package list with DNF
sudo dnf upgrade	Upgrade all packages with DNF
sudo dnf remove <package_name>	Remove a package with DNF
sudo yum install <package_name>	Install a package with YUM (older systems)

Adding a Repository

To add a custom repository to DNF/YUM, create a new file in the `/etc/yum.repos.d/` directory.

```
sudo tee /etc/yum.repos.d/example.repo <<EOF
[example]
name=Example Repository
baseurl=http://example.com/repository
enabled=1
gpgcheck=1
gpgkey=http://example.com/repository/RPM-GPG-KEY-example
EOF

sudo dnf update
```

Zypper - SUSE-based Systems

Zypper is the package manager for openSUSE and SUSE Linux Enterprise. It offers a powerful command-line interface with advanced features like dependency resolution and repository management.

Command	Description
sudo zypper install <package_name>	Install a package
sudo zypper refresh	Update package list
sudo zypper update	Upgrade all packages
sudo zypper remove <package_name>	Remove a package

Adding a Repository

To add a custom repository to Zypper, use the `addrepo` command.

```
sudo zypper addrepo
http://download.opensuse.org/repositories/example/repo/ example-repo
sudo zypper refresh
```

Pacman - Arch Linux

Pacman is the package manager for Arch Linux, known for its simplicity and speed. It uses binary packages and a simple package format to manage software.

Command	Description
sudo pacman -S <package_name>	Install a package
sudo pacman -Syu	Update package list and upgrade all packages
sudo pacman -R <package_name>	Remove a package

Adding a Repository

To add a custom repository to Pacman, edit the `/etc/pacman.conf` file and add the repository details.

```
sudo tee -a /etc/pacman.conf <<EOF
[example-repo]
SigLevel = Optional TrustAll
Server = http://example.com/repository/$arch
EOF

sudo pacman -Syu
```

Linux Security

Linux security involves multiple layers of defense including network security, application security, and system integrity measures. These layers work together to protect the system from unauthorized access, vulnerabilities, and attacks. Key tools in Linux security include AppArmor, Firewalld, Lynis, and Fail2ban.

Linux security provides several benefits, including improved system integrity, protection against unauthorized access, and enhanced monitoring and auditing capabilities. By implementing these security measures, administrators can safeguard sensitive data, ensure compliance with security policies, and maintain a stable and secure operating environment. Practical examples of Linux security benefits include preventing unauthorized access through strict access controls, mitigating potential vulnerabilities with regular audits, and dynamically managing network traffic to protect against external threats.

AppArmor

AppArmor (Application Armor) is a Linux security module that provides mandatory access control (MAC) to restrict the capabilities of programs. It uses profiles to define what resources and privileges a program can access, effectively limiting the potential damage from compromised applications.

Installation

To install AppArmor on a Debian system (e.g., Ubuntu), use the following commands:

```
sudo apt update
sudo apt install apparmor apparmor-utils
sudo systemctl enable --now apparmor
```

To install AppArmor on RHEL (Red Hat Enterprise Linux), use the following commands:

```
sudo dnf update
sudo dnf install apparmor apparmor-utils
sudo systemctl enable --now apparmor
```

Common App Armor Commands

Command	Description
aa-status	Displays the current status of AppArmor profiles.
aa-enforce <profile>	Enforces the specified AppArmor profile.
aa-complain <profile>	Sets the specified profile to complain mode (logs violations instead of enforcing them).
aa-logprof	Scans log files for AppArmor events and helps create or update profiles.
aa-unconfined	Lists unconfined processes and their potential risks.

Firewalld

Firewalld is a dynamic firewall daemon that provides a user-friendly way to manage network security. It supports network zones, which define the trust level of network connections and can be configured to allow or restrict traffic based on these zones.

Installation

To install Firewalld on a Debian system (e.g., Ubuntu), use the following commands:

```
sudo apt update
sudo apt install firewalld
sudo systemctl enable --now firewalld
```

To install Firewalld on RHEL (Red Hat Enterprise Linux), use the following commands:

```
sudo dnf update
sudo dnf install firewalld
sudo systemctl enable --now firewalld
```

Common Firewalld Commands:

Command	Description
firewall-cmd –state	Checks the state of the Firewalld service.
firewall-cmd –get-active-zones	Lists all active zones and interfaces associated with them.
firewall-cmd –zone=<zone> --add-service=<service>	Adds a service to a specific zone.
firewall-cmd –zone=<zone> --add-port=<port>/tcp	Adds a port to a specific zone.
firewall-cmd –reload	Reloads the Firewalld configuration without disconnecting established connections.

Lynis

Lynis is a security auditing tool for Unix-based systems. It performs an extensive health scan of the system to identify potential security issues and provide suggestions for hardening.

Installation

To install Lynis on a Debian system (e.g., Ubuntu), use the following commands:

```
sudo apt update
sudo apt install lynis
```

To install Lynis on RHEL (Red Hat Enterprise Linux), use the following commands:

```
sudo dnf update
sudo dnf install lynis
```

Common Lynis Commands:

Command	Description
lynis audit system	Performs a full system audit and generates a report.
lynis show audit	Displays details about the last audit performed.
lynis update info	Checks for available updates for Lynis.
lynis check all	Runs all available tests and checks.
lynis configure	Helps configure Lynis settings and preferences.

Fail2ban

Fail2ban is a log-parsing utility that scans log files for failed login attempts and bans offending IP addresses by updating firewall rules. It helps protect against brute-force attacks and other malicious activities.

Installation

To install Fail2ban on a Debian system (e.g., Ubuntu), use the following commands:

```
sudo apt update
sudo apt install fail2ban
sudo systemctl enable --now fail2ban
```

To install Fail2ban on RHEL (Red Hat Enterprise Linux), use the following commands:

```
sudo dnf update
sudo dnf install fail2ban
sudo systemctl enable --now fail2ban
```

Commond Fail2ban Commands:

Command	Description
fail2ban-client status	Shows the status of the Fail2ban service and configured jails.
fail2ban-client status <jail>	Shows detailed status for a specific jail.
fail2ban-client set <jail> banip <ip>	Manually bans an IP address for a specific jail.
fail2ban-client set <jail> unbanip <ip>	Manually unbans an IP address for a specific jail.
fail2ban-regex <logfile> <regex>	Tests regular expressions against log file entries to ensure proper configuration.

Services / Daemons

Nix has two general types of processes: foreground and background. Foreground processes take control of the user's terminal, meaning the terminal cannot be used for other commands until the process completes. Examples of foreground processes include text editors such as emacs, vim, or nano.

Background processes, on the other hand, run without user interaction and do not take control of the terminal. These can be launched by appending an "&" after the command, which pushes the process into the background. This allows the terminal to be used for other commands while the background process continues to run. To bring a background process to the foreground, the "fg" command can be used. Additionally, the jobs command can be used to list background processes, and "bg" can be used to resume a stopped job in the background.

Init

In traditional Linux, the System V init (SysVinit) process used the /etc/inittab configuration file to drive the execution of init scripts and the configuration of terminal and GUI interfaces. SysVinit launches scripts and daemon processes one at a time, in order, based on the runlevel configuration found in /etc/rc.#. The disadvantage of the SysVinit boot procedure is that it is based on runlevel directories that contain a massive number of scripts, all of which have to be started sequentially. This can result in slower boot times and less efficient resource utilization.

SysVinit has been largely replaced by Upstart and systemd in many Linux distributions. Upstart introduced event-based initialization, allowing for more flexible and responsive process management.

Systemd, which has become the most common replacement, introduces the concept of systemd units. Systemd units are configuration files that describe services, sockets, devices, mounts, automounts, swap, targets, paths, timers, and snapshots. Systemd improves upon SysVinit by enabling parallel service startup, reducing boot time, and providing more advanced features such as on-demand starting of daemons, dependency management, and a powerful system monitoring and management tool.

SysVinit uses a set of initialization scripts located in /etc/init.d/ or /etc/rc.d/ to manage daemons. These scripts are executed sequentially according to the system's runlevel, defined in /etc/inittab. Different operating modes, known as runlevels, determine which services are started or stopped. Each daemon has an associated script in /etc/init.d/ that defines how to start, stop, and restart the service. Symbolic links in directories like /etc/rc3.d/ point to these scripts, determining the order of service startup and shutdown.

Systemd

Systemd is a system and service manager for Linux operating systems. It is designed to be backward compatible with SysV init scripts and provides a number of advanced features. These features include parallel startup of system services at boot time, on-demand activation of daemons, support for system state snapshots, and dependency-based service control logic.

Systemd also introduces the concept of "units," which are configuration files that define how services, sockets, devices, mounts, automounts, swap, targets, paths, timers, and snapshots should be managed. This enables more efficient resource utilization, improved system performance, and greater flexibility in managing system services and processes.

Systemd is a modern system and service manager that replaces SysVinit in many Linux distributions. It provides more advanced features and greater efficiency in managing daemons. Systemd uses unit files to define services, sockets, devices, mounts, and more. These files are typically located in /etc/systemd/system/ or /usr/lib/systemd/system/. Service units (.service) define how to manage a daemon, including commands to start, stop, and reload the service. Socket units (.socket) define network or IPC sockets that systemd listens on for socket-based activation. Target units (.target) group multiple units to form a specific system state, similar to runlevels.

Systemd commands include systemctl start <service> to start a service, systemctl stop <service> to stop a service, systemctl restart <service> to restart a service, systemctl enable <service> to enable a service to start at boot, systemctl disable <service> to disable a service from starting at boot, and systemctl status <service> to show the status of a service. Systemd can start multiple services simultaneously, significantly reducing boot times. Units can specify dependencies, ensuring services start in the correct order, and systemd can start services when needed rather than at boot, improving resource utilization.

Upstart

Upstart is an event-based replacement for the /sbin/init daemon, which handles starting tasks and services during boot, stopping them during shutdown, and supervising them while the system is running. The "init" or "system initialization" process on Unix and Linux systems has process ID (PID) "1". This means it is the first process to start when the system boots (ignoring the initrd/initramfs). Upstart improves upon traditional init systems by using events to trigger tasks and services, allowing for more dynamic and efficient management of system processes.

Runlevels

Linux has 7 default runlevels, which can be thought of as 7 different operating modes. These modes are not run one after the other but rather represent different states that the system can be in at any given point. Each runlevel has its own list of settings for which services to start and which services to shut down. This list includes not only the services that should be running but also the order in which each service should be started.

Runlevel 0 halts the system, while runlevel 1 is single-user mode used for administrative tasks and maintenance. Runlevel 2 is multi-user mode without networking, and runlevel 3 is multi-user mode with networking in text mode. Runlevel 4 is undefined and user-definable, while runlevel 5 is multi-user mode with networking and a graphical user interface (GUI). Finally, runlevel 6 reboots the system.

Each runlevel has its own directory within /etc/rc.d/ (or /etc/init.d/ depending on the distribution) that contains symbolic links to the scripts that should be run when entering or leaving the runlevel. The order in which services are started or stopped is determined by the naming convention of these symbolic links, usually prefixed with 'K' for kill (stop) and 'S' for start, followed by a number indicating the sequence.

Runlevel	Generic	Fedora	Slackware	Debian
0	halt	halt	halt	halt
1	single-usermode	single-usermode	single-usermode	single-usermode
2	basic multi-user (no networking)	user definable	user definable (default same as runlevel 3)	multi-user mode
3	full multi-user mode	multi-user mode	multi-user mode (Default)	
4	not used	not used	X11 with session managers	multi-user mode
5	full GUI multi-user mode	full multi-user X based (Default)	user definable (default same as runlevel 3)	
6	reboot	reboot	reboot	reboot

Daemons

Daemons are background processes that run continuously and independently of user interactions. They are crucial for the system's operation, performing various tasks such as handling network requests, managing hardware, executing scheduled tasks, and logging system events. Typically, daemons do not have a direct user interface and operate silently, providing essential services that support the overall functionality of the Linux operating system. Daemons run in the background, detached from any terminal session, and start at system boot, running continuously until the system is shut down. They operate independently of direct user control, often providing services that other applications and users depend on. Daemons conventionally have names ending in 'd' (e.g., `sshd`, `httpd`), signifying their role as background services.

List of Common Daemons

This list categorizes various daemons found in Unix-like operating systems into sections based on their primary functions. Daemons are background processes that provide essential system services.

System Management Daemons

System Management Daemons are responsible for handling core system operations and administrative tasks. These daemons manage system logging, task scheduling, power management, and system monitoring. They ensure that the system runs smoothly by automating routine tasks, managing resources, and providing critical system services. Understanding these daemons is essential for system administrators to maintain and optimize the performance of a Unix-like operating system.

Daemon	Function
amd	Auto Mount Daemon. Automatically mounts file systems on demand.
anacron	Executes delayed cron tasks at boot time. Ensures scheduled tasks are run even if the system was off.
apmd	Advanced Power Management Daemon. Manages power-related tasks, particularly on older hardware.
atd	Runs jobs queued using the at tool. Schedules one-time tasks to be executed at a specific time.
auditd	Linux Audit Daemon. Collects and writes audit logs for system security monitoring.
autofs	Supports the automounter daemon, allowing mount and unmount of devices on demand.
crond	Task Scheduler Daemon. Runs scheduled tasks defined in crontab.
cupsd	CUPS (Common Unix Printing System) printer daemon. Manages print jobs and printers.
memcached	In-memory distributed object caching daemon. Speeds up dynamic web applications by caching data in RAM.
mysql	Database server daemon. Provides database services using MySQL.
postgresql	Database server daemon. Provides database services using PostgreSQL.
rsyslogd	Message Logging Daemon. Collects and logs system messages locally and remotely.
syslogd	System logging daemon. Collects and logs system messages.
syncd	Keeps the file system synchronized with system memory.
webmin	Web-based administration server daemon. Provides a web interface for system administration.

Network Services Daemons

Network Services Daemons manage network-related functions and services. These daemons handle network configuration, time synchronization, web serving, and network security. They are crucial for maintaining network connectivity, managing IP addresses, providing remote access, and ensuring that network services are running efficiently. Knowledge of these daemons is vital for network administrators to configure and troubleshoot network operations in Unix-like systems.

Daemon	Function
dhcpd	Dynamic Host Configuration Protocol daemon. Assigns IP addresses to devices on a network.
gated	Routing daemon that handles multiple routing protocols and replaces routed and egpup.
httpd	Web server daemon. Serves web pages over HTTP.
inetd	Internet supervisor daemon. Manages network services like FTP, telnet, and others.
network-manager	Network Manager Daemon. Simplifies network configuration and management.
ntpd	Network Time Protocol daemon. Synchronizes the system clock with network time servers.
rpcbind	Remote Procedure Call Bind daemon. Maps RPC program numbers to IP address and port number combinations.
squid	Web page caching proxy server daemon. Speeds up web browsing by caching web pages.
sshd	Secure Shell (SSH) server daemon. Provides secure remote login and command execution.
telnetd	Telnet server daemon. Provides remote login services via the Telnet protocol.
xinetd	Enhanced internet supervisor daemon. Manages network services with more features than inetd.
xntpd	Network Time Protocol (NTP) server daemon. Synchronizes the system clock with network time servers.

File and Print Services Daemons

File and Print Services Daemons are responsible for managing file sharing, printing, and related services. These daemons provide and manage access to file systems over networks, handle printing tasks, and support various file transfer and email protocols. They are essential for ensuring seamless file and print services in multi-user environments. Understanding these daemons helps administrators set up and maintain efficient file and print services for users.

Daemon	Function
ftpd	FTP server daemon. Provides file transfer protocol services.
imapd	IMAP server daemon. Provides email retrieval services via the IMAP protocol.
lpd	Line Printer Daemon. Manages print jobs for printers using the LPD protocol.
mountd	Mount daemon. Manages NFS mount requests from clients.
named	DNS (Domain Name System) server daemon. Resolves domain names to IP addresses.
nfsd	Network File System daemon. Shares files and directories over a network.
nfslock	NFS file locking services. Ensures file consistency in NFS environments.
nmbd	Network Message Block daemon. Provides NetBIOS over IP naming services to clients.
postfix	Mail transport agent. A replacement for sendmail, used for routing and delivering email.
routed	Routing table daemon. Manages the routing tables on a network.
sendmail	Mail transfer agent daemon. Routes and delivers email.
smbd	Samba (SMB) daemon. Provides file and print services to SMB/CIFS clients.
smtpd	Simple Mail Transfer Protocol daemon. Manages email sending and receiving.
snmpd	Simple Network Management Protocol daemon. Collects and processes network data for network management.
tcpd	Service wrapper. Restricts access to services managed by inetd using hosts.allow and hosts.deny.
vsftpd	Very Secure File Transfer Protocol daemon. A secure and fast FTP server.

Daemon Commands using Service

The `service` command provides a standardized way to control daemons on systems using SysVinit and offers backward compatibility for systems that have transitioned to Systemd. It ensures consistent daemon management across different initialization systems.

Command	Description
service <daemon> start	Starts the specified daemon.
service <daemon> stop	Stops the specified daemon.
service <daemon> restart	Restarts the specified daemon.
service <daemon> reload	Reloads the configuration of the specified daemon without stopping it.
service <daemon> status	Displays the current status of the specified daemon.
service <daemon> enable	Enables the daemon to start at boot time (note: primarily Systemd specific).
service <daemon> disable	Disables the daemon from starting at boot time (note: primarily Systemd specific).
service –status-all	Lists the status of all available services.

Using systemctl Command (Systemd):

The `systemctl` command allows administrators to start, stop, restart, and check the status of services, among other functions. It is essential for managing daemons and ensuring system services run as expected.

Command	Description
systemctl start <service>	Starts the specified service.
systemctl stop <service>	Stops the specified service.
systemctl restart <service>	Restarts the specified service.
systemctl reload <service>	Reloads the configuration of the specified service without stopping it.
systemctl status <service>	Displays the current status of the specified service.
systemctl enable <service>	Enables the service to start at boot time.
systemctl disable <service>	Disables the service from starting at boot time.
systemctl is-enabled <service>	Checks if the specified service is enabled.
systemctl is-active <service>	Checks if the specified service is active (running).
systemctl daemon-reload	Reloads the systemd manager configuration.
systemctl mask <service>	Masks a service to prevent it from being started.
systemctl unmask <service>	Unmasks a service to allow it to be started.

OS Shell

The shell is an interactive interface that allows users to execute commands and utilities in Linux and other UNIX-based operating systems. The shell is also referred to as the terminal. When you open the terminal, most modern systems will be executing /bin/bash, which means the Bash shell. However, you can also use /bin/sh, which traditionally means the Bourne shell. On Linux distributions, /bin/sh is often a symbolic link to either /bin/bash or the Dash shell. Despite this, in general, /bin/sh historically refers to the Bourne shell.

The shell provides a command-line interface (CLI) where users can type commands to perform various tasks such as file manipulation, program execution, and system administration. There are several types of shells available, each with its own features and capabilities: Bash (Bourne Again Shell), the default shell on many Linux distributions, known for its advanced scripting features and compatibility with the Bourne shell; Dash (Debian Almquist Shell), a POSIX-compliant shell often used as /bin/sh for its speed and efficiency; Zsh (Z Shell), known for its powerful scripting, customization options, and advanced features such as spell correction and theme support; Ksh (Korn Shell), a shell compatible with the Bourne shell, offering many enhancements and features for scripting and interactive use; and Fish (Friendly Interactive Shell), a user-friendly shell with features like syntax highlighting, autosuggestions, and a web-based configuration interface.

Bash (Bourne Again Shell)

Bash is the default shell on many Linux distributions and is an enhanced version of the original Bourne shell (sh). It is widely used for its advanced scripting features and compatibility with the Bourne shell.

Benefits:

- Compatibility: Fully compatible with Bourne shell scripts.
- Scripting Features: Offers powerful scripting capabilities, including functions, arrays, and string manipulation.
- Interactive Use: Provides features like command history, tab completion, and aliasing.

Bash includes numerous enhancements over the original Bourne shell, such as improved programming constructs, job control, and command-line editing. It also offers more scripting capabilities and interactive features compared to simpler shells like Dash.

Dash (Debian Almquist Shell)

Dash is a POSIX-compliant shell often used as /bin/sh for its speed and efficiency. It is a minimalistic shell designed to be fast and lightweight.

Benefits:

- Speed: Faster execution of scripts compared to Bash.
- Efficiency: Uses fewer system resources, making it suitable for system scripts and embedded systems.
- POSIX Compliance: Adheres strictly to POSIX standards, ensuring portability of scripts.

Differences:
Dash lacks many of the interactive and scripting features found in Bash. It is designed to be small and efficient, making it less suitable for interactive use and more appropriate for script execution.

Zsh (Z Shell)

Zsh is known for its powerful scripting capabilities, customization options, and advanced interactive features. It is highly extensible and user-friendly.

Benefits:

- Customization: Highly customizable with support for themes and plugins.
- Advanced Features: Includes spell correction, improved tab completion, and powerful globbing.
- Scripting: Supports all features of Bourne shell and more, making it excellent for complex scripts.

Zsh offers more advanced features compared to Bash, such as better auto-completion and customization options. It is also more user-friendly with features like spelling correction and enhanced history capabilities.

Ksh (Korn Shell)

Ksh is a shell compatible with the Bourne shell, offering numerous enhancements and features for both scripting and interactive use. It was developed by David Korn.

Benefits:

- Compatibility: Compatible with Bourne shell scripts.
- Enhanced Features: Includes advanced scripting features like associative arrays and built-in arithmetic operations.
- Interactive Use: Offers job control, command-line editing, and a robust history mechanism.

Ksh provides more scripting features than Bash and is considered more powerful for certain scripting tasks. It strikes a balance between Bash's simplicity and Zsh's advanced features.

Fish (Friendly Interactive Shell)

Fish is a user-friendly shell with features like syntax highlighting, autosuggestions, and a web-based configuration interface. It aims to be interactive and easy to use.

Benefits:

- User-Friendly: Offers an intuitive user experience with syntax highlighting and autosuggestions.
- Configuration: Provides a web-based configuration interface for easy setup.
- Interactive Features: Includes powerful interactive features like command history search and tab completion.

Fish prioritizes user-friendliness and ease of use over POSIX compatibility, making it less suitable for running traditional POSIX shell scripts. However, it excels in providing an enhanced interactive shell experience.

Linux Common Directories and Configuration Files

Common Linux Directories

Directory	Description
/	Root Directory
/bin	Binaries
/boot	Boot Files (Kernel)
/dev	System Devices
/etc	Config Files
/home	User Directory
/lib	Software Libraries
/media	Mount Points
/mnt	Temporary Mount Point
/opt	3rd Party Software
/proc	Processes
/root	Root Home Directory
/run	Run time variables
/sbin	Admin Binaries
/tmp	Temporary Files
/usr	User Binaries, Libraries
/var	Variable System Files

Common Linux Config Files

Directory	Description
/etc/shadow	Hashes of users password
/etc/passwd	Local Users
/etc/group	Local Groups
/etc/fstab	Mounting Paritions
/etc/rc.d	runcom startup
/etc/init.d	service scripts
/etc/hosts	Local DNS
/etc/HOSTNAME	hostname for localhost
/etc/network/interfaces	Network Config File
/etc/profile	System Environment Variables
/etc/apt/sources.list	Package sources for APT-GET
/etc/resolv.conf	DNS Servers
~/.bash_history	User Bash History
~/.ssh	SSH Authorized Keys
/var/log	System Log Files
/var/adm	
/var/log/apache/access.log	Apache Connection Log

Dot File	Description
.bash_login	Used if .bash_profile does not exist
.bash_logout	Used by bash shells at exit
.bash_profile	Used by bash after /etc/profile
.bash_history	List of commands used previously
.profile	Used if ~/.bash_profile and .bash_login don't exist
.vimrc	Default VIM configuration file
.emacs	Read by Emacs at startup

Linux System Information

This table lists common Linux commands along with their descriptions. These commands are used for a variety of tasks such as checking system information, managing processes, and handling packages.

Linux Network Commands

Command	Description
host <ip>	Get the hostname for the specified IP address.
who am i	Display the current user.
w	Show logged in users and their activities.
who -a	Show detailed information about all users.
last -a	Show user login history, including the hostname or IP address of the user.
ps	Display currently running processes.
df	Display free disk space on all mounted filesystems.
uname -a	Show kernel and OS version information.
mount	Show all currently mounted filesystems.
getent passwd	Get entries from the passwd database (user information).
PATH=$PATH:/<directory>	Add the specified directory to the PATH environment variable.
kill <pid>	Terminate the process with the specified PID (Process ID).
kill -9 <pid>	Forcefully terminate the process with the specified PID.
cat /etc/issue	Display a system identification message or OS information.
cat /etc/release	Display distribution-specific release information (e.g., /etc/lsb-release).
cat /proc/version	Show kernel version information.
rpm -i *.rpm	Install an RPM package.
rpm -qa	Show all installed RPM packages.
dpkg -i *.deb	Install a DEB package.
dpkg –get-selections	Show a list of installed DEB packages.
pkginfo	Show installed packages on Solaris systems.
cat /etc/shells	Display the locations of all available shell executables.
chmod -x <shell dir>	Make the specified shell directory non-executable.

The ifconfig and ip commands are both used for network configuration on Linux systems but they have important differences. ifconfig is part of the older net-tools suite and has been widely used for many years to configure network interfaces, set IP addresses, and manage routing tables. However, ifconfig is now deprecated in favor of the ip command, which is part of the iproute2 package. The ip command provides more advanced capabilities and flexibility.

The ip command provides a comprehensive suite of tools for network management. It can handle tasks related to IP addresses, routes, network interfaces, tunnels, and much more, all in a unified syntax. For example, to assign an IP address, ifconfig would use ifconfig <interface> <ip>/<cidr>, while the ip equivalent is ip addr add <ip>/<cidr> dev <interface>. To set a default gateway, ifconfig uses route add default gw <ip>, whereas ip uses ip route add default via <ip>.

One of the major advantages of ip is its ability to provide more detailed information and finer control over network configurations. The ip command supports modern networking features that ifconfig does not, such as multiple IP addresses per interface, network namespaces, and more sophisticated routing rules. Additionally, ip provides clearer and more structured output, which is helpful for both beginners and advanced users.

For beginners, transitioning from ifconfig to ip might seem challenging at first, but learning ip is essential as it is the current standard for network configuration in Linux. Advanced users benefit from the extensive functionality and scriptability of ip, allowing for more complex and efficient network management tasks.

Command	Description
watch ss -tp	Monitor TCP connections continuously
netstat -an(t)(u)	Display (t)TCP and (u)UDP connections
netstat -anop	Display network connections with PID
lsof -i	List established network connections
smb://<ip>/<sharename>	Access Windows SMB share
share <user> <ip> c$	Mount Windows share
smbclient -U <user> \\\\<ip>\\<sharename>	Connect to SMB share
ifconfig <interface> <ip>/<cidr>	Set IP address and network mask (deprecated, use ip addr add)
ifconfig <interface>:1 <ip>/<cidr>	Set virtual interface IP address (deprecated, use ip addr add)
route add default gw <ip>	Set default gateway (deprecated, use ip route add)
ifconfig <interface> mtu <mtu size>	Set MTU size (deprecated, use ip link set mtu)
ip addr add <ip>/<cidr> dev <interface>	Set IP address and network mask
ip addr add <ip>/<cidr> dev <interface> label <interface>:1	Set virtual interface IP address
ip route add default via <ip>	Set default gateway
ip link set <interface> mtu <mtu size>	Set MTU size
macchanger -m <mac> <interface>	Change MAC address
iwlist <interface> scan	Scan for WiFi networks
dig -x <ip>	Lookup domain by IP
host <ip>	
host -t <type> <server>	Lookup specific DNS record type
dig @<ip> <domain> -t AXFR	Perform DNS zone transfer
host -l <domain> <namesrv>	List DNS records for a domain
ip xfrm state list	Print VPN keys
tcpkill host <ip> and port <port>	Block traffic to/from a specific IP and port
echo "1" > /proc/sys/net/ipv4/ip_forward	Enable IP forwarding
echo "nameserver <ip>" >> /etc/resolv.conf	Add DNS server

Linux Basic and Administrative Commands

Command	Description
sudo	Execute command as superuser
curl <url>	Get HTML of a webpage
wget <url>	Retrieve a file from the web
rdesktop <ip>	Connect to a remote desktop
ssh <user>@<ip>	Secure Shell for remote login
scp <source> <user>@<ip>:<destination>	Securely copy file to remote host
scp <user>@<ip>:<source> <destination>	Securely copy file from remote host
useradd <username>	Add a new user
passwd <user>	Change user password
rmuser <user>	Remove a user
script -a <outfile>	Record terminal session
apropos <topic>	Search manual pages for topic
history	Show command history
! <number>	Execute command from history by number
env	Display environment variables
top	Show system's top processes
ifconfig	Display network interface information (deprecated, use ip)
ip addr show	Show IP addresses and properties
ip link show	Show network interfaces
lsof	List open files associated with a process
df	Report filesystem disk space usage
du	Estimate file space usage
mount	Mount a filesystem
umount	Unmount a filesystem
service <service> start	Start a service
service <service> stop	Stop a service
service <service> restart	Restart a service
systemctl <action> <service>	Control the systemd system and service manager

Graphics Server

The X Window System (X11) has been the standard graphical server for Unix-like operating systems since the 1980s, providing a network-transparent window system that enables applications to run on one machine while displaying on another. X11 operates on a client-server model where the X server manages the display and input devices, and X clients are the applications requesting graphical operations. This architecture, while flexible and powerful, introduces latency due to its indirect rendering path, even for local applications. X11 supports numerous extensions like GLX for OpenGL rendering and XRender for advanced 2D graphics, but its complexity and legacy codebase make maintenance challenging. Moreover, the security model of X11, designed in an earlier era, can be prone to vulnerabilities.

Wayland, in contrast, is a modern graphics server protocol designed to address the shortcomings of X11 by providing a simpler and more efficient architecture. Wayland eliminates the separate window manager by integrating compositing into the display server, resulting in direct communication between the compositor and clients, which reduces latency and improves performance. This streamlined protocol enhances security with isolated input/output channels, reducing the risk of application eavesdropping. Despite its benefits, Wayland faces compatibility challenges as many applications and toolkits are still dependent on X11, necessitating compatibility layers like XWayland. While Wayland is gaining traction, its adoption is not yet universal, and some advanced features available in X11 are still being implemented.

X11

The X Window System (X11, or simply X) is a windowing system for bitmap displays, commonly found on Unix-like operating systems. X provides the basic framework for a graphical user interface (GUI) environment, enabling the drawing and moving of windows on the display device and facilitating interaction with a mouse and keyboard.

X operates on a client-server model. The X server manages the display, handling input from the keyboard and mouse and output to the screen. X clients are the applications that communicate with the server to request graphical operations. One of the most powerful features of X is its network transparency, allowing applications to run on a remote machine while displaying the output locally. This means you can run a program on one computer and view and interact with it on another. X is highly extensible, supporting a wide range of hardware devices and graphical capabilities, including extensions like GLX (OpenGL Extension to the X Window System) for 3D graphics.

X relies on window managers to control the placement and appearance of windows since it does not manage windows itself. Popular window managers include Metacity, Compiz, and Openbox. Some modern desktop environments like GNOME, KDE, and Xfce integrate their own window managers. The X server is the central component that communicates with the hardware (display, keyboard, mouse) and handles all the graphical output. X clients are applications that use the X protocol to request windowing operations from the X server. Display managers manage user sessions and logins, typically launching the X server and initial client applications. Examples include GDM (GNOME Display Manager) and LightDM. Window managers control the appearance and behavior of windows, handling window borders, title bars, and controls like maximize, minimize, and close buttons.

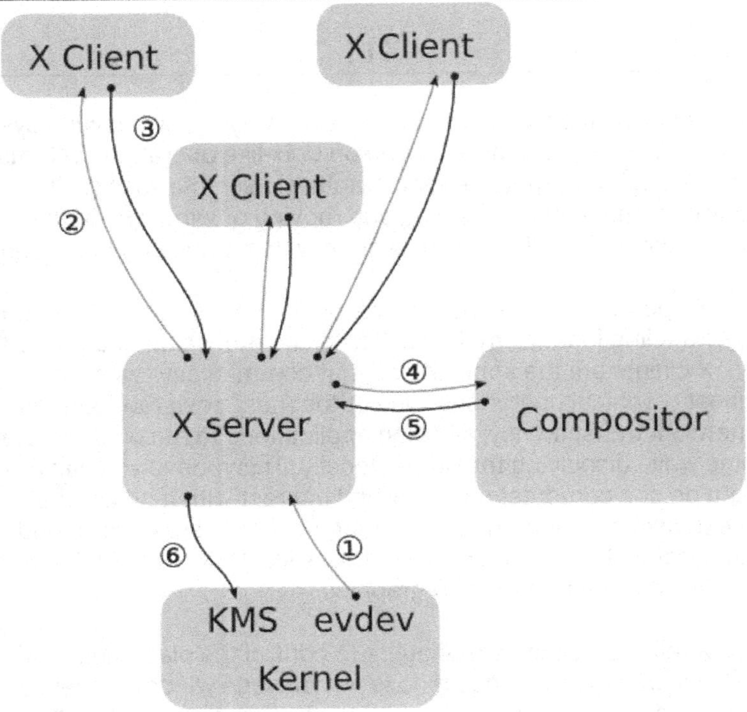
X Client
X Client
③
X Client
②
④
X server
⑤
Compositor
⑥
①
KMS
evdev
Kernel

Wayland

Wayland is a communication protocol that specifies the interaction between a display server and its clients, as well as a C library implementation of that protocol. A display server using the Wayland protocol is called a Wayland compositor because it also performs the task of a compositing window manager. Unlike the X Window System, where the display server and window manager are separate, Wayland integrates these functions into a single, cohesive unit, resulting in a simpler and potentially more efficient architecture.

Wayland offers several key features. Its simplified architecture reduces complexity and overhead by combining the display server and compositing window manager into one component. This integration can improve performance and responsiveness by minimizing the number of context switches and enabling direct rendering. Additionally, Wayland enhances security by isolating clients more effectively than X, reducing the potential for certain types of exploits. It also takes advantage of modern graphics hardware features, delivering smoother and more consistent graphical performance.

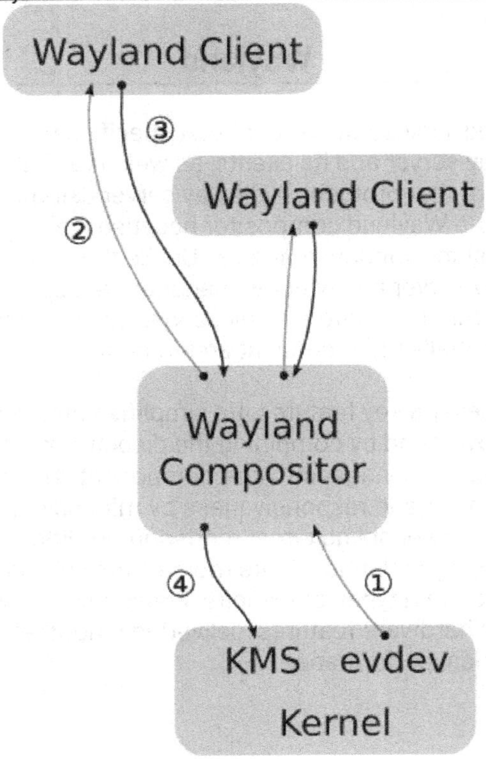
Wayland Client
③
Wayland Client
②
Wayland Compositor
④
①
KMS
evdev
Kernel

Common Wayland commands:

Command/Tool	Description
weston	Reference Wayland compositor. Starts a Wayland session using Weston.
sway	A popular tiling Wayland compositor compatible with i3 configuration.
wayland-info	Displays information about the Wayland environment and its components.
WAYLAND_DISPLAY	Environment variable specifying the Wayland display socket.
weston-launch	Launches the Weston compositor with elevated privileges.
wlr-randr	Utility for configuring display settings on Wayland (part of wlroots).
weston-terminal	Terminal emulator for Weston.
wl-copy	Command-line tool to copy data to the Wayland clipboard.
wl-paste	Command-line tool to paste data from the Wayland clipboard.

Desktop Environments

KDE

Overview

KDE stands for K Desktop Environment. It is a popular desktop environment for Linux-based operating systems, known for its configurability, rich set of features, and vibrant community. KDE offers a visually appealing and user-friendly interface with a variety of applications designed to enhance productivity and user experience.

- **File Manager**: Dolphin – A powerful and flexible file manager.
- **Web Browser**: Konqueror – A versatile web browser and file manager.
- **Office Suite**: KOffice – A lightweight office suite, though many users now prefer LibreOffice for a more feature-rich experience.
- **Remote Desktop**: KRDC – A user-friendly remote desktop client.
- **Bittorrent Client**: KTorrent – A comprehensive and easy-to-use bittorrent client.

Debian

KDE Full

```
sudo apt install kde-full
```

KDE Standard

```
sudo apt install kde-standard
```

KDE Plasma Desktop

```
sudo apt install kde-plasma-desktop
```

Fedora/CentOS

```
sudo dnf groupinstall -y "KDE Plasma Workspaces"
```

OR use deprecated YUM

```
yum groupinstall 'KDE'
```

GNOME

Overview

GNOME is a free and open-source desktop environment for Unix-like operating systems. Initially, GNOME stood for GNU Network Object Model Environment, but this acronym was later dropped as it no longer aligned with the project's vision. GNOME focuses on simplicity, ease of use, and accessibility, offering a clean and intuitive user interface.

- **File Browser**: Nautilus – A streamlined file manager designed for simplicity.
- **Web Browser**: Web (formerly known as Epiphany) – A simple, clean, and fast web browser.
- **Remote Desktop**: Connections – A modern and easy-to-use remote desktop client.
- **Bittorrent Client**: Transmission – A lightweight and efficient bittorrent client.

Debian

```
sudo apt install gnome-session gdm3
```

Fedora/CentOS

```
sudo dnf install @gnome-desktop
```

Cinnamon

Overview

Cinnamon is a free and open-source desktop environment for the X Window System. It is derived from GNOME 3 but adheres to traditional desktop metaphor conventions, providing a familiar and intuitive interface for users who prefer a classic desktop layout.

File Browser: Nemo
Web Browser: Chromium
Remote Desktop: Connections
Bittorrent: Transmission

Debian

```
sudo apt install cinnamon
```

Fedora/CentOS

```
sudo dnf groupinstall -y "Cinnamon Desktop"
```

XFCE

Overview

Xfce, also stylized as XFCE, is a free and open-source desktop environment for Unix-like operating systems. Xfce aims to be fast and lightweight while still being visually appealing and easy to use. It embodies the traditional Unix philosophy of modularity and reusability, providing a robust environment without unnecessary bloat.

File Browser: Thunar
Office Suite: Text Editor

Debian

```
sudo apt-get install xubuntu-desktop
```

Fedora/CentOS

```
sudo dnf groupinstall -y "Xfce Desktop"
```

Linux Virtualization

Virtualization Technologies

Virtualization allows running multiple operating systems on a single physical machine, providing significant benefits in terms of resource utilization, isolation, and management. Key technologies in virtualization include KVM, QEMU, and Xen.

Virtualization provides several benefits, including improved resource utilization, isolation, security, management, and flexibility. It maximizes the use of physical hardware by running multiple virtual machines, leading to cost savings by reducing the need for physical servers. Virtual machines are isolated from each other, enhancing security and stability, and virtualization offers a secure environment for running applications, reducing the risk of system-wide compromises. Virtualization simplifies the management of multiple virtual machines compared to physical servers and allows for easy creation, modification, and deletion of virtual machines as needs change. Practical examples of virtualization benefits include enhanced disaster recovery capabilities through easy backup and restoration of virtual machines and improved load balancing by distributing workloads across multiple virtual machines.

KVM

KVM (Kernel-based Virtual Machine) is a virtualization module integrated into the Linux kernel that allows it to function as a hypervisor. It supports native virtualization using hardware extensions provided by Intel VT-x and AMD-V. KVM offers near-native performance due to direct execution on hardware, supports multiple virtual CPUs and large amounts of memory, and integrates seamlessly with other Linux tools and distributions. Common use cases for KVM include server consolidation, where multiple server workloads run on a single physical server, and creating isolated environments for software development and testing.

Installation:

To install KVM on a Debian system (e.g., Ubuntu), use the following commands:

```
sudo apt update
sudo apt install qemu-kvm libvirt-daemon-system libvirt-clients
bridge-utils virt-manager
sudo systemctl enable --now libvirtd
sudo usermod -aG libvirt $(whoami)
```

To install KVM on RHEL (Red Hat Enterprise Linux), use the following commands:

```
sudo yum update
sudo yum install qemu-kvm libvirt libvirt-daemon libvirt-daemon-
config-network libvirt-daemon-kvm bridge-utils virt-manager
sudo systemctl enable --now libvirtd
sudo usermod -aG libvirt $(whoami)
```

Command	Description
virsh list	List all active virtual machines.
virsh start <vm>	Start a specified virtual machine.
virsh shutdown <vm>	Shut down a specified virtual machine.
virsh destroy <vm>	Forcefully stop a specified virtual machine.
virsh create <xml>	Create and start a virtual machine from an XML configuration file.
virsh edit <vm>	Edit the configuration of a specified virtual machine.
virsh snapshot-create <vm>	Create a snapshot of a specified virtual machine.
virsh snapshot-list <vm>	List all snapshots of a specified virtual machine.
virsh console <vm>	Connect to the console of a specified virtual machine.
virt-install	Install a new virtual machine using a command-line tool.
virt-manager	GUI tool for managing virtual machines.

QEMU

QEMU (Quick EMUlator) is an open-source machine emulator and virtualizer. It can perform hardware virtualization using KVM or operate as a stand-alone emulator. QEMU is highly flexible, capable of emulating a wide range of hardware architectures, and can function as both a hypervisor with KVM and a standalone emulator. It also supports snapshotting, allowing users to take snapshots of virtual machines for backup and recovery. This makes QEMU ideal for cross-platform virtualization, running software designed for different hardware architectures, and emulating entire systems for education, development, and testing purposes.

Installation:

To install QEMU on a Debian system (e.g., Ubuntu), use the following commands:

```
sudo apt update
sudo apt install qemu qemu-kvm libvirt-daemon-system libvirt-clients
bridge-utils virt-manager
```

To install QEMU on RHEL (Red Hat Enterprise Linux), use the following commands:

```
sudo yum update
sudo yum install qemu-kvm libvirt libvirt-daemon libvirt-daemon-
config-network libvirt-daemon-kvm bridge-utils virt-manager
```

Command	Description
qemu-system-x86_64 -hda <img>	Start a virtual machine using the specified disk image.
qemu-img create -f qcow2 <img> <size>	Create a new disk image in QCOW2 format.
qemu-img convert -O <format> <src> <dest>	Convert a disk image to a different format.
qemu-snapshot -c <name>	Create a snapshot of the current state of the virtual machine.
qemu-snapshot -l	List all snapshots of the virtual machine.
qemu-monitor	Access the QEMU monitor for advanced commands and debugging.
qemu-bridge-helper	Helper for configuring bridge networking.
qemu-system-x86_64 -m <size> -smp <n>	Start a VM with specified memory size and number of CPU cores.
qemu-system-x86_64 -cdrom <iso>	Boot a virtual machine from a specified ISO image.

XEN

Xen is an open-source hypervisor that enables the creation, management, and execution of multiple virtual machines on a single physical system. It uses a microkernel design, separating the hypervisor from the host operating system. Xen is known for its strong isolation between virtual machines and high performance due to its lightweight design. It supports paravirtualization, which allows for more efficient operation of guest systems. Xen is widely used in cloud computing environments to provide virtualized infrastructure and in high-performance computing to run performance-critical applications in isolated environments.

Installation:

To install Xen on a Debian system (e.g., Ubuntu), use the following commands:

```
sudo apt update
sudo apt install xen-hypervisor-amd64 xen-tools
```

To install Xen on RHEL (Red Hat Enterprise Linux), use the following commands:

```
sudo yum update
sudo yum install xen xen-tools
sudo systemctl enable xen
sudo systemctl start xen
```

Command	Description
xl list	List all running virtual machines.
xl create <config>	Create and start a virtual machine using a configuration file.
xl shutdown <vm>	Shut down a specified virtual machine.
xl destroy <vm>	Forcefully stop a specified virtual machine.
xl console <vm>	Connect to the console of a specified virtual machine.
xl save <vm> <file>	Save the state of a virtual machine to a file.
xl restore <file>	Restore a virtual machine from a saved state file.
xl migrate <vm> <host>	Migrate a virtual machine to another host.
xl snapshot-create <vm>	Create a snapshot of a specified virtual machine.
xl snapshot-list <vm>	List all snapshots of a specified virtual machine.
xl dmesg	Display Xen hypervisor messages.

Nix Filesystems

In Unix-like operating systems, such as Linux, all filesystems have a single root directory denoted by "/", from which all folders and files are structured into a hierarchical tree. To the Linux kernel, the filesystem is represented as a collection of inodes, which are fundamental components in Linux filesystems. Understanding inodes and their components is essential for both beginners and advanced users to manage and interact with the filesystem effectively.

Each file in Linux comprises three primary components: the dentry (directory entry), inode, and data. The dentry represents the filename and facilitates the mapping between the filename and the inode. The inode is a crucial structure that contains metadata about the file, while the data component is where the actual contents of the file are stored. Each inode has a unique identifier within the filesystem known as the inode number, which allows the kernel to efficiently manage and access file metadata.

Inodes store several critical pieces of information. They maintain ownership details, as every file in Linux has a user owner and a group owner. Each owner is associated with three different permission levels: read (r), write (w), and execute (x). These permissions determine the level of access granted to the file's owners and other users. Additionally, inodes keep track of three different timestamps: atime (access time), ctime (change time), and mtime (modification time). Atime updates and records the last time the file was accessed, ctime updates whenever the inode information changes, and mtime updates when the file's actual data is modified.

Moreover, inodes store two measurements related to file size: file length and file size. File length refers to the actual number of bytes in the file, whereas file size indicates the amount of disk space consumed by the file. This can vary due to factors such as filesystem block size and file system overhead. Understanding this distinction is particularly important for comprehending storage utilization and optimizing disk usage. The block size, which is the smallest unit of storage allocation on the disk, can affect both the performance and the amount of wasted space due to internal fragmentation.

In addition to metadata and size information, inodes manage links, which are crucial for filesystem operations. There are two types of links: hard links and soft (symbolic) links. A hard link assigns multiple dentries (filenames) to a single inode, allowing different filenames to reference the same physical data on the disk. This is useful for creating backup copies of files without duplicating the data. Conversely, a soft link is a distinct inode that references another dentry (filename). This is akin to shortcuts in other operating systems and allows for flexible file management across different directories or filesystems. Hard links enhance data redundancy and save space, while soft links offer flexibility in organizing and accessing files.

Understanding these components and their interactions is fundamental for both system administrators and users aiming to optimize their use of Linux filesystems. For beginners, grasping the concept of inodes and permissions is crucial for effective file management and security. For advanced users, in-depth knowledge of inode structures, timestamps, and links is vital for tasks such as troubleshooting, optimizing storage, and performing advanced filesystem operations. This comprehensive understanding of filesystems in Linux thus provides a robust foundation for managing, securing, and optimizing Linux environments.

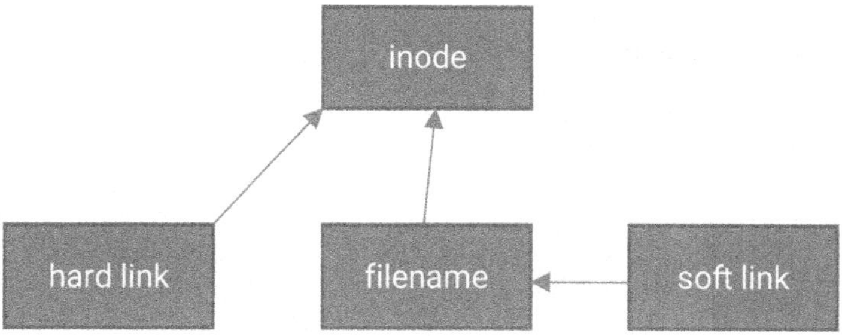

Permission Types

Permission	Symbol	Description
read	r	The Read permission refers to a user's capability to read the contents of the file.
write	w	The Write permissions refer to a user's capability to write or modify a file or directory.
execute	x	The Execute permission affects a user's capability to execute a file or view the contents of a directory.

Permission Modes

Access Class	Operator	Description
u (user)	+ (Add)	Adds specified permission Example: (chmod +x <file>)
g (group)	- (Revoke)	Removes specified permission Example: (chmod -x <file>)
o (other)	= (Assign)	Assigns specified permission Example: (chmod u=x <file>)

Permission Octal Values

Octal Digit	Binary Representation (rwx)	Permission
0	0	none
1	1	execute only
2	10	write only
3	11	write and execute
4	100	read only
5	101	read and execute
6	110	read and write
7	111	read, write, and execute (full permissions)

Remote Access

SSH

Option	Description
-1	Instructs ssh to use protocol version 1.
-2	Instructs ssh to use protocol version 2.
-4	Permits only IPv4 addresses.
-6	Permits only IPv6 addresses.
-A	Enables authentication agent connection forwarding. Use this option with caution.
-a	Disables authentication agent connection forwarding.
-b bind_address	Sets the source address of the connection on a host with multiple network interfaces.
-C	Enables data compression for all files. Use this with slow connections.
-c cipher_spec	Selects a cipher specification. List values separated by commas.
-D [bind_address:]port	Specifies a local "dynamic" application-level port forwarding.
-E log_fileName	Attaches debug logs to log_file instead of standard error.
-f	Sends ssh to the background before authentication.
-g	Permits remote hosts to connect to ports forwarded on the local machine.
-i identity_file	Selects a file from which the identity (private key) for public key authentication is read.
-J destination	Specifies a jump host for the connection. This uses a proxy command to connect via another host.
-k	Disables GSSAPI authentication and forwarding.
-L [bind_address:]port:host:hostport	Specifies a local port forwarding.
-M	Places ssh into master mode for connection sharing.
-N	Do not execute a remote command. Useful for forwarding ports.
-O ctl_cmd	Sends a control command to the ssh multiplexing master process.
-p port	Specifies the port to connect to on the remote host.
-q	Runs ssh in quiet mode. Suppresses most error or warning messages.
-R [bind_address:]port:host:hostport	Specifies a remote port forwarding.
-S ctl_path	Specifies the location of a control socket for connection sharing.
-T	Disables pseudo-tty allocation.
-t	Forces pseudo-tty allocation.
-V	Displays the version of the ssh tool and exits.
-v	Prints debugging messages for the ssh connection. Verbose mode is useful for troubleshooting.
-X	Enables X11 forwarding.
-x	Disables X11 forwarding.
-Y	Enables trusted X11 forwarding.
-y	Sends log information to the system logger.

Samba

Samba is a suite of programs that enable a Linux system to communicate with the Microsoft Server Message Block (SMB) protocol. SMB is used by Microsoft for file sharing and printer services. Samba allows Linux systems to share files and printers with Windows systems, making it a crucial tool in mixed-OS environments. Introduced in 1992, Samba has become a key component in providing seamless interoperability between Linux and Windows, especially in corporate networks. Samba also supports Active Directory (AD) integration, which allows Linux servers to participate in AD domains, providing authentication and directory services.

Samba Daemons

1. **smbd**: The Samba server daemon that manages services such as resource sharing, resource locking, user authentication, and user authorization. This daemon uses TCP port 445. It is responsible for providing file and print services to SMB/CIFS clients and handling authentication and authorization of users.
2. **nmbd**: The NetBIOS server daemon that handles services such as browsing file shares, print shares available on the network, and hostname resolution. This daemon uses UDP ports 137 for NetBIOS name service, 138 for NetBIOS datagram service, and 139 for NetBIOS session service. It is responsible for ensuring that the Samba server can be found by other computers on the network through NetBIOS name resolution.

Configuration

The default configuration file for Samba is `smb.conf`, located at `/etc/samba/smb.conf`. This file is divided into sections, each of which contains specific configuration options:

- **[global]**: Configure server-specific options. This section contains settings that affect the overall behavior of the Samba server. Typical configurations include specifying workgroup name, enabling or disabling logging, setting security levels, and more.
- **[homes]**: Configure home directory share options. This section is typically used to dynamically provide home directories to users. Each user's home directory can be accessed when they log in, enhancing the ease of access and security of personal files.
- **[printers]**: Configure printer-specific options. This section is used to manage printer shares. You can specify printer paths, set printing permissions, and control the availability of printers over the network.

Testing Samba Configuration

To test Samba configuration and ensure that the syntax is correct, use the `testparm` utility. This tool checks the `smb.conf` file for syntax errors and provides a summary of the current configuration. The command is as follows:

```
testparm /etc/samba/smb.conf
```

Running this command will validate the configuration file and display any errors or warnings that need to be addressed, ensuring that your Samba server operates smoothly.

Security Practices

Securing your Samba server is crucial, especially in mixed-OS environments. Common practices include:

- Using strong passwords and changing them regularly.
- Limiting access to shares by configuring user and group permissions.
- Regularly updating Samba to the latest version to protect against vulnerabilities.
- Using firewalls to restrict access to Samba services.

By following these practices, you can ensure that your Samba server remains secure and efficient in providing file and printer sharing services across different operating systems.

Field	Description
workgroup	Name of the Windows workgroup or domain.
netbios name	Name of the Samba server.
server string	Description that identifies the Samba server.
interfaces	Network address for the Samba server, specified as a list of interfaces/IP addresses to bind.
hosts allow / deny	Allows or denies hosts from specified networks, using CIDR notation or specific IP addresses.
log file	Defines the log file name for each client, with variables such as %m to create unique log files.
max log size	Size in KB for the log file before it is rotated.
security	Selects the authentication mode: 1. ADS - Active Directory 2. Domain – Domain controller 3. Server – Uses another Samba server 4. Share – Users do not have server authentication 5. User (default) – Users authenticate locally.
passdb backend	Selects the backend for authentication: 1. smbpasswd - Uses /var/lib/samba/private/smbpasswd files 2. tdbsam – Creates a local TDB database in /var/lib/samba 3. ldapsam – Uses a remote LDAP server.
realm	Name of the Active Directory realm, required for Kerberos authentication.
password server	Name of the server used for network authentication, often specified for ADS security.
local master	Specifies if the server will try to become the local master browser on the subnet.
os level	Determines the precedence of the Samba server in master browsing elections (higher is preferred).
preferred master	Specifies whether to force a local browser election on startup.
wins support	Specifies whether to enable WINS support, acting as a WINS server.
load printers	Specifies whether to load the list of printers automatically from the system.
comment	Description or comment about the share, visible to clients.
browseable	Instructs the SMB client whether the share should be listed in browse lists.
path	Sets the absolute path to the directory being shared.
valid users	Specifies a list of users and groups who are allowed access to the share.
writeable	Specifies if the share is writable. Equivalent options include: 1. read only = no 2. writeable = yes 3. writable = yes 4. write ok = yes.
create mask	Sets local file permissions for any new files created within the share.
directory mask	Sets local file permissions for any new directories created within the share.

Samba Browsing Config Options

Option	Function
announce as	Sets the operating system that Samba will announce itself as (e.g., Windows NT).
announce version	Sets the version of the operating system that Samba will announce itself as.
browseable (browsable)	Allows the share to be displayed in the list of machine resources.
browse list	If yes, Samba will provide a browse list on this server.
auto services (preload)	Sets a list of shares that will always appear in the browse list.
default service (default)	Names a share (service) that will be provided if the client requests a share not listed in smb.conf.
local master	If yes, Samba will try to become a master browser on the local subnet.
lm announce	Enables or disables LAN Manager style host announcements.
lm interval	Specifies the frequency in seconds that LAN Manager announcements will be made if activated.
preferred master (prefered master)	If yes, Samba will use the preferred master browser bit to attempt to become the local master browser.
domain master	If yes, Samba will try to become the main browser master for the workgroup.
os level	Sets the operating system level of Samba in an election for local master browser.
remote browse sync	Lists Samba servers to synchronize browse lists with.
remote announce	Lists subnets and workgroups to send directed broadcast packets to, allowing Samba to appear in browse lists.

Samba Variables

Samba includes a comprehensive set of variables for determining the characteristics of the Samba server and the clients to which it connects. These variables, which begin with a percent sign followed by a single uppercase or lowercase letter, can only be used on the right side of a configuration option (e.g., after the equal sign). They allow for dynamic configuration based on various conditions and parameters.

Variable	Definition
Client variables	
%a	Client's architecture (e.g., Samba, WfWg, WinNT, Win95, or UNKNOWN)
%I	Client's IP address (e.g., 192.168.220.100)
%m	Client's NetBIOS name
%M	Client's DNS name
User variables	
%g	Primary group of %u
%G	Primary group of %U
%H	Home directory of %u

%u	Current Unix username
%U	Requested client username (not always used by Samba)
Share variables	
%p	Automounter's path to the share's root directory, if different from %P
%P	Current share's root directory
%S	Current share's name
Server variables	
%d	Current server process ID
%h	Samba server's DNS hostname
%L	Samba server's NetBIOS name
%N	Home directory server, from the automount map
%v	Samba version
Miscellaneous variables	
%R	The SMB protocol level that was negotiated
%T	The current date and time

Samba Config Tips

Samba Configuration Tips

Proper configuration of Samba can significantly impact its performance, security, and maintainability. Here are some essential tips for optimizing and managing your Samba server:

Optimizing Performance

Adjusting the `socket options` parameter in `smb.conf` can optimize performance for different network environments. For example:

```
socket options = TCP_NODELAY SO_RCVBUF=8192 SO_SNDBUF=8192
```

- **TCP_NODELAY**: This option disables Nagle's algorithm, which can reduce latency for network communications.
- **SO_RCVBUF and SO_SNDBUF**: These options set the buffer size for receiving and sending data, respectively. Adjusting these values can improve throughput, especially in high-latency networks.

Experimenting with these values based on your specific network environment can lead to noticeable performance improvements.

Enhancing Security

Ensure the `security` parameter is set appropriately based on your network environment. This parameter determines how clients authenticate to the server:

- **security = user**: This setting is suitable for standalone servers where users authenticate with a username and password.
- **security = ads**: This setting is used for Active Directory integration, providing centralized authentication and enhanced security.

Selecting the appropriate security mode helps balance functionality and security, ensuring that only authorized users can access shared resources.

Logging and Auditing

Use the `log level` parameter to increase the verbosity of logging for troubleshooting purposes:

```
log level = 3
```

- **log level**: Setting this parameter to a higher value increases the detail of logs. For example, `log level = 3` provides detailed logs useful for debugging but can impact performance if set too high.

Higher log levels generate more detailed information, which is invaluable for diagnosing issues but can affect server performance. It's advisable to increase the log level temporarily while troubleshooting and revert to a lower level during normal operation.

Backup and Restore

Regularly back up the `smb.conf` file and associated TDB/LDAP databases, especially when using advanced configurations like `passdb backend = ldapsam`.

- **Backing up `smb.conf`**: Copy the configuration file to a secure location regularly.

```
cp /etc/samba/smb.conf /backup/smb.conf.bak
```

Backing up TDB/LDAP databases: Use appropriate tools to back up databases. For TDB, you can use the `tdbbackup` utility:

```
tdbbackup /var/lib/samba/passdb.tdb
```

Regular backups ensure that you can quickly restore your configuration in case of corruption or accidental changes, maintaining the integrity and availability of your Samba services.

FTP

The File Transfer Protocol (FTP) provides a standard network protocol for transferring files between a client and a server on a computer network. FTP is widely used for uploading files to a server, downloading files from a server, and managing file systems remotely. It operates on the client-server model, utilizing separate control and data connections between the client and server.

Command	Description
mdir	Displays a list of a remote directory's files and subdirectories
mget	Copies one or more remote files to the local computer
mkdir	Creates a remote directory
mls	Displays an abbreviated list of a remote directory's files and subdirectories
mput	Copies one or more local files to the remote computer
open	Connects to the specified FTP server
prompt	Toggles prompting (default = ON)
put	Copies a single local file to the remote computer
pwd	Displays the current directory on the remote computer (literally, "print working directory")
quit	Ends the FTP session with the remote computer and exits ftp (same as "bye")
quote	Sends arguments, verbatim, to the remote FTP server (same as "literal")
recv	Copies a remote file to the local computer
remotehelp	Displays help for remote commands
rename	Renames remote files
rmdir	Deletes a remote directory
send	Copies a local file to the remote computer (same as "put")
status	Displays the current status of FTP connections
trace	Toggles packet tracing (default = OFF)
type	Sets or displays the file transfer type (default = ASCII)
user	Specifes a user to the remote computer
verbose	Toggles verbose mode (default = ON)

Command	Description
!	Runs the specified command on the local computer
?	Displays descriptions for ftp commands
append	Appends a local file to a file on the remote computer
ascii	Sets the file transfer type to ASCII, the default
bell	Toggles a bell to ring after each file transfer command is completed (default = OFF)
binary	Sets the file transfer type to binary
bye	Ends the FTP session and exits ftp
cd	Changes the working directory on the remote computer
close	Ends the FTP session and returns to the command interpreter
debug	Toggles debugging (default = OFF)
delete	Deletes a single file on a remote computer
dir	Displays a list of a remote directory's files and subdirectories
disconnect	Disconnects from the remote computer, retaining the ftp prompt
get	Copies a single remote file to the local computer
glob	Toggles filename globbing (wildcard characters) (default = ON)
hash	Toggles hash sign (#) printing for each data block transferred (default = OFF)
help	Displays descriptions for ftp commands
lcd	Changes the working directory on the local computer
literal	Sends arguments, verbatim, to the remote FTP server
ls	Displays an abbreviated list of a remote directory's files and subdirectories
mdelete	Deletes one or more files on a remote computer

Linux Automation

Automation tools streamline repetitive tasks and improve system management efficiency. They enable administrators to define infrastructure as code, ensuring consistency, reducing human error, and speeding up deployment processes. Popular tools include Ansible, Puppet, and Chef.

Automation provides several benefits, including improved consistency, scalability, and reliability in managing IT infrastructure. By automating routine tasks, administrators can focus on more strategic initiatives, reducing the risk of errors and ensuring that configurations are applied uniformly across all systems. Automation tools also facilitate rapid scaling of infrastructure, making it easier to manage a large number of servers or virtual machines. Additionally, they provide a centralized way to manage configurations and deployments, enhancing security and compliance. Practical examples of automation benefits include automated software deployments, configuration management, and orchestration of complex workflows.

Ansible

Ansible is an open-source automation tool that uses simple, human-readable YAML syntax to define tasks. It operates over SSH, requiring no agent installation on the client systems. Ansible is known for its ease of use and its ability to quickly and efficiently automate complex tasks.

Installation

To install Ansible on a Debian system (e.g., Ubuntu), use the following commands:

```
sudo apt update
sudo apt install ansible
```

To install Ansible on RHEL (Red Hat Enterprise Linux), use the following commands:

```
sudo yum update
sudo yum install ansible
```

Command	Description
ansible <hosts> -m <module>	Run a specific Ansible module on the specified hosts.
ansible-playbook <playbook>	Execute a playbook with defined tasks.
ansible-inventory --list	List the inventory of hosts and groups.
ansible-galaxy install <role>	Install a role from Ansible Galaxy.
ansible-doc <module>	Display documentation for a specific module.

Example Script to Install Apache:

```
---
- name: Install and start Apache web server
  hosts: webservers
  become: yes
  tasks:
    - name: Install Apache
      apt:
        name: apache2
        state: present
      when: ansible_os_family == 'Debian'

    - name: Install Apache
      yum:
        name: httpd
        state: present
      when: ansible_os_family == 'RedHat'

    - name: Start Apache service
      service:
        name: "{{ (ansible_os_family == 'Debian') |
ternary('apache2', 'httpd') }}"
        state: started
        enabled: yes
```

To run example playbook

```
ansible-playbook -i inventory.ini apache_install.yml
```

Puppet

Puppet is a configuration management tool that uses a declarative language to describe the desired state of infrastructure. It uses a client-server model where the Puppet master server manages configurations and the Puppet agents apply these configurations on the client systems.

Installation

To install Puppet on a Debian system (e.g., Ubuntu), use the following commands:

```
wget https://apt.puppetlabs.com/puppet-release-bionic.deb
sudo dpkg -i puppet-release-bionic.deb
sudo apt update
sudo apt install puppet-agent
```

To install Puppet on RHEL (Red Hat Enterprise Linux), use the following commands:

```
sudo rpm -Uvh https://yum.puppetlabs.com/puppet-release-el-
7.noarch.rpm
sudo yum update
sudo yum install puppet-agent
```

Command	Description
puppet agent --test	Run the Puppet agent to apply configurations from the Puppet master.
puppet apply <manifest>	Apply Puppet configurations defined in a manifest file locally.
puppet module install <module>	Install a module from the Puppet Forge.
puppet resource <type> <name>	Inspect and manipulate resources on the system.
puppet config print	Print Puppet configuration settings.

Example Puppet Script to Deploy Apache:

```
class apache {
  package { 'apache2':
    ensure => installed,
  }

  service { 'apache2':
    ensure     => running,
    enable     => true,
    require    => Package['apache2'],
  }
}

if $facts['os']['family'] == 'RedHat' {
  class { 'apache':
    package { 'httpd':
      ensure => installed,
    }

    service { 'httpd':
      ensure     => running,
      enable     => true,
      require    => Package['httpd'],
    }
  }
} else {
  class { 'apache': }
}
```

Apply Script:

```
sudo puppet apply apache.pp
```

Chef

Chef is an automation tool that uses a Ruby-based DSL to define infrastructure as code. It follows a client-server architecture, with the Chef server managing configurations and the Chef clients applying these configurations. Chef is designed to be highly flexible and scalable.

Installation

To install Chef on a Debian system and RHEL, use the following command:

```
curl -L https://omnitruck.chef.io/install.sh | sudo bash
```

Command	Description
chef-client	Run the Chef client to apply configurations from the Chef server.
knife bootstrap <node>	Bootstrap a node to be managed by Chef.
knife node list	List all nodes managed by the Chef server.
knife cookbook create <name>	Create a new Chef cookbook.
chef-shell	Start an interactive Chef shell for debugging and development.

Example Chef Script to install apache

```
# apache.rb

if platform_family?('debian')
  package 'apache2' do
    action :install
  end

  service 'apache2' do
    action [:enable, :start]
  end
elsif platform_family?('rhel')
  package 'httpd' do
    action :install
  end

  service 'httpd' do
    action [:enable, :start]
  end
end
```

Chef install and run cookbook

```
chef generate cookbook my_cookbook
cd my_cookbook
mkdir -p recipes
sudo chef-client --local-mode --runlist 'recipe[my_cookbook::apache]'
```

Web Servers

Web servers are critical components in the infrastructure of web applications. They handle requests from clients, serve web pages, and manage various web-related services. This section covers four of the most widely-used web servers: Nginx, Tomcat, Apache and LiteSpeed. Each of these servers has unique features and strengths, making them suitable for different use cases and environments.

HTTP Status Codes

100s HTTP Informational Codes	
100	Continue
101	Switching Protocols
102	Processing
103	Checkpoint
122	Request-URI too long
200s HTTP Successful Codes	
200	OK
201	Created
202	Accepted
203	Non-Authoritative Information
204	No Content
205	Reset Content
206	Partial Content
207	Multi-Status
208	Already Reported
226	IM Used
300s HTTP Redirection Codes	
300	Multiple Choices
301	Moved Permanently
302	Found

303	See Other
304	Not Modified
305	Use Proxy
306	Switch Proxy
307	Temporary Redirect
400s HTTP Client Error Code	
400	Bad Request
401	Unauthorized
402	Payment Required
403	Forbidden
404	Not Found
405	Method Not Allowed
406	Not Acceptable
407	Proxy Authentication Required
408	Request Timeout
409	Conflict
410	Gone
411	Length Required
412	Precondition Failed
413	Request Entity Too Large
414	RequestURI Too Long
415	Unsupported Media Type
416	Requested Range Not Satisfiable
417	Expectation Failed
418	I'm a teapot
422	Unprocessable Entity
423	Locked
424	Failed Dependency
425	Unordered Collection
426	Upgrade Required
428	Precondition Required

429	Too Many Requests
431	Request Header Fields Too Large
444	No Response
449	Retry With
450	Blocked By Windows Parental Controls
451	Unavailable For Legal Reasons
499	Client Closed Request
	500s HTTP Server Error Codes
500	Internal Server Error
501	Not Implemented
502	Bad Gateway
503	Service Unavailable
504	Gateway Timeout
505	HTTP Version Not Supported
506	Variant Also Negotiates
507	Insufficient Storage
508	Loop Detected
509	Bandwidth Limit Exceeded
510	Not Extended
511	Network Authentication Required
598	Network read timeout error
599	Network connect timeout error

Apache

Apache HTTP Server, commonly referred to as Apache, is a widely-used open-source web server software. Apache is known for its flexibility, robustness, and extensive feature set, making it a popular choice for hosting websites and applications. It supports various functionalities through modules, including URL redirection, authentication, and SSL/TLS encryption.

Listen Port:

Changing the listen port of Apache is necessary when you want to run the server on a port other than the default (port 80 for HTTP and port 443 for HTTPS). This can be useful for running multiple web servers on the same machine or for security purposes.

Debian

```
# Change /etc/apache2/ports.conf
Listen <port>
# Also change /etc/apache2/sites-enabled/000-default.conf
<VirtualHost *:<port>>
…
<VirtualHost>
```

CentOS/RHEL

```
# Change /etc/httpd/conf/httpd.conf
Listen <port>
```

Change document root

Changing the document root allows you to specify the directory from which Apache serves files. This is important when hosting multiple websites or organizing your web content in different directories.

```
<VirtualHost *:80>
ServerAdmin webmaster@<domain>.com
ServerName <domain>.com
ServerAlias www.<domain>.com
# Change the DocumentRoot to the path for your html
DocumentRoot /var/www/<website directory>
# Set options for your html directory
<Directory /var/www/<website directory> >
Options Indexes FollowSymLinks MultiViews
AllowOverride All
Require all granted
allow from all
```

```
</Directory>
# Set Logs to the directory of your html
ErrorLog /var/www/<website directory> /error.log
CustomLog /var/www/<website directory> /access.log combined
</VirtualHost><span style="font-weight: 400;">
```

Enable HTTPS (using certbot)

Enabling HTTPS ensures secure communication between the client and the server, protecting data integrity and confidentiality. Using Certbot, you can easily obtain and install SSL certificates from Let's Encrypt.

```
sudo apt install python-certbot-apache
sudo certbot --apache
sudo certbot --apache -d example.com -d www.example.com
```

Renew HTTPS cron

Regularly renewing your HTTPS certificates is crucial to maintaining secure connections. Automating this process with a cron job ensures that your certificates are always up-to-date.

```
sudo crontab -e
### Add the below line ###
30 0 * * * /usr/bin/certbot renew
```

Restrict by IP or subnet

Restricting access by IP or subnet enhances security by allowing only specific clients to access your server. This is particularly useful for internal applications or administrative interfaces.

```
<Location />
  Order deny,allow
  Deny from all
  # Allow from single IP
  Allow from XXX.XXX.XXX.XXX
  # Allow from subnet
  Allow from YYY.YYY.YYY.0/24
  # Deny from single IP
  Deny from XXX.XXX.XXX.XXX
  #Deny from subnet
  Deny from YYY.YYY.YYY.0/24
</Location>
```

Web root for apache is located at /var/www/html/

Directory	Description
/etc/httpd/conf/httpd.conf or /etc/apache2/apache2.conf	Standard Apache web server configuration file
/etc/httpd/conf.d/ssl.conf or /etc/apache2/ssl.conf	Secure Apache web server configuration file for SSL/TLS settings
/etc/httpd/conf.d/*.conf	Configuration files for supporting services and modules
.htaccess	Directory-level configuration file for specific content served by Apache
/etc/httpd/conf.modules.d/*.conf	Configuration files for loading Apache modules
/etc/httpd/conf/magic	File type mappings used by mod_mime_magic
/etc/httpd/logs/	Directory containing Apache log files
/etc/httpd/run/	Directory containing runtime data, such as PID files
/etc/httpd/conf/extra/	Additional configuration files for specific features or extensions

Nginx

Nginx is open-source software used for web serving, reverse proxying, caching, load balancing, media streaming, mail proxy, and HTTP cache. Created by Igor Sysoev and publicly released in 2004, Nginx has grown in popularity due to its performance and reliability. It is free and open-source software, released under the terms of the 2-clause BSD license. Nginx is known for its high performance, stability, rich feature set, simple configuration, and low resource consumption, making it a preferred choice for many developers and system administrators.

Install:

To install Nginx, you need to update your package lists and install the Nginx package using your distribution's package manager. Below are the commands for CentOS/RHEL and Debian-based systems.

CentOS/RHEL

```
sudo yum update
sudo yum install nginx
sudo nginx -v
```

Debian

```
sudo apt-get update
sudo apt-get install nginx
sudo nginx -v
```

Common configurations for nginx.

Nginx configurations are defined in files that usually reside in `/etc/nginx/`. The main configuration file is `nginx.conf`, and additional configurations can be included in this file using the `include` directive.

Listen to port:

You can configure Nginx to listen on different ports and protocols, including IPv4 and IPv6. This is essential for setting up HTTP and HTTPS services.

```
server {
  # Standard HTTP Protocol
```

```
  listen 80;

  # Standard HTTPS Protocol
  listen 443 ssl;

  # Listen on 80 using IPv6
  listen [::]:80;

  # Listen only on using IPv6
  listen [::]:80 ipv6only=on;
}
```

Access Logging:

Access logs are crucial for monitoring traffic and diagnosing issues. You can configure the location and verbosity of the access logs.

```
server {
  # Relative or full path to log file
  access_log /path/to/file.log;

  # Turn 'on' or 'off'
  access_log on;
}
```

Domain Name:

You can specify the domain names that Nginx should respond to using the `server_name` directive. This helps in hosting multiple domains on the same server.

```
server {
  # Listen to yourdomain.com
  server_name yourdomain.com;

  # Listen to multiple domains
  server_name yourdomain.com www.yourdomain.com;

  # Listen to all domains
  server_name *.yourdomain.com;

  # Listen to all top-level domains
  server_name yourdomain.*;

  # Listen to unspecified Hostnames (Listens to IP address itself)
  server_name "";

}
```

Static Assets:

Nginx can be configured to serve static assets directly, improving performance by offloading this task from your application server.

```
server {
  listen 80;
  server_name yourdomain.com;

  location / {
          root /path/to/website;
  }
}
```

Redirects:

Redirects are useful for SEO and ensuring users are directed to the correct version of your site (e.g., redirecting www to non-www).

```
server {
  listen 80;
  server_name www.yourdomain.com;
  return 301 http://yourdomain.com$request_uri;
}
```

```
server {
  listen 80;
  server_name www.yourdomain.com;

  location /redirect-url {
     return 301 http://otherdomain.com;
  }
}
```

Reverse Proxy:

Nginx can act as a reverse proxy, forwarding requests to another server. This is commonly used to balance the load or provide an additional layer of security.

```
server {
  listen 80;
  server_name yourdomain.com;

  location / {
     proxy_pass http://0.0.0.0:3000;
     # where 0.0.0.0:3000 is your application server (Ex: node.js)
bound on 0.0.0.0 listening on port 3000
  }

}
```

Load Balancing:

Load balancing distributes traffic across multiple servers to ensure no single server becomes overwhelmed, improving reliability and performance.

```
upstream node_js {
```

```
  server 0.0.0.0:3000;
  server 0.0.0.0:4000;
  server 123.131.121.122;
}

server {
  listen 80;
  server_name yourdomain.com;

  location / {
     proxy_pass http://node_js;
  }
}
```

SSL

Configuring SSL ensures secure communication between the client and server. Nginx supports SSL/TLS for encrypting HTTP traffic.

```
server {
  listen 443 ssl;
  server_name yourdomain.com;

  ssl on;

  ssl_certificate /path/to/cert.pem;
  ssl_certificate_key /path/to/privatekey.pem;

  ssl_stapling on;
  ssl_stapling_verify on;
  ssl_trusted_certificate /path/to/fullchain.pem;

  ssl_protocols TLSv1 TLSv1.1 TLSv1.2;
  ssl_connection_timeout 1d;
  ssl_session_cache shared:SSL:50m;
  add_header Strict-Transport-Security max-age=15768000;
}

# Permanent Redirect for HTTP to HTTPS
server {
  listen 80;
  server_name yourdomain.com;
  return 301 https://$host$request_uri;
}
```

Tomcat

Apache Tomcat is an open-source implementation of the Java Servlet, JavaServer Pages (JSP), and WebSocket technologies. It is widely used as a servlet container and web server for running Java applications. Tomcat is known for its simplicity, flexibility, and ease of use, making it a popular choice for both development and production environments.

Version Specifications

Different versions of Tomcat support various specifications of Java technologies, providing developers with the necessary features for building and deploying web applications.

- **Tomcat 8.0.x**: Supports Servlet 3.1, JSP 2.3, EL 3.0, WebSocket 1.1, and requires Java 7 and later. This version provides enhanced asynchronous processing, improved security features, and better support for modern web protocols.
- **Tomcat 7.0.x**: Supports Servlet 3.0, JSP 2.2, EL 2.2, WebSocket 1.1, and requires Java 6 and later (WebSocket requires Java 7). It introduces support for annotations, asynchronous servlets, and improved memory management.
- **Tomcat 6.0.x**: Supports Servlet 2.5, JSP 2.1, EL 2.1, and requires Java 5 and later. This version focuses on stability and compatibility with older Java specifications.

Tomcat provides various commands to manage its server operations. Here are some commonly used commands:

Command	Description
debug [-security]	Starts in a debugger
start [-security]	Starts in a separate window (or in the background)
run [-security]	Starts in the current window (in the foreground)
stop [-force]	Stops server waiting up to 5 seconds -force option kills the process if not stopped after 5 seconds
jpda start	Starts under JPDA debugger – Environment variable JPDA_ADDRESS defines the debug address (often just a port) and JPDA_SUSPEND to suspend execution immediately after start-up
version	Displays the Tomcat version.
configtest	Checks the configuration files for errors.

Tomcat's architecture comprises various components, each serving a specific role in handling requests and managing resources.

Name	Role
Server	The server (aggregate instance) and admin configuration (mainly shutdown socket definition) and hierarchy.
Listener	Tomcat internal events listener (see org.apache.catalina.LifecycleListener).
GlobalNamingResources	Defines a set of container-wide resources (as opposed to application-specific ones).
Resource	Defines a JNDI resource.
Service	A set of connectors and an engine.
Connector	Defines a protocol to use and its configuration (most common ones are HTTP and AJP).
Engine	The processor of an incoming request from a connector; includes a pipeline starting from the host, going through authentication if needed, the webapp, and finally the servlet.
Executor	The thread pool associated with a Service to handle requests.
Realm	Security repository (login/password/roles); 0 or 1 can be linked to Host, Engine, and/or Context.
Host	Virtual host representation ("domain"); a container of Contexts (explicit or implicit using appBase).
Context	A web application.
Valve	An element of the request pipeline (can be added to Engine, Host, or Context).

LiteSpeed

LiteSpeed Web Server (LSWS) is a high-performance, secure, and scalable web server designed to handle thousands of concurrent connections with minimal memory and CPU usage. It is often used as a drop-in replacement for Apache due to its compatibility with Apache's configurations and enhanced performance. LiteSpeed supports various features, including HTTP/2, SSL/TLS, and caching, making it an excellent choice for modern web applications and high-traffic websites.

To install LiteSpeed on a Linux system, you need to download the installation script and run it with superuser privileges. Below are the steps for a typical installation.

```
wget https://www.litespeedtech.com/packages/5.0/lsws-5.4.10-ent-
x86_64-linux.tar.gz
tar -zxvf lsws-5.4.10-ent-x86_64-linux.tar.gz
cd lsws-5.4.10
sudo ./install.sh
```

Listening to Ports

You can configure LiteSpeed to listen on different ports to handle HTTP and HTTPS traffic.

```
listener Default {
  address                    *:80
  secure                     0
}

listener SSL {
  address                    *:443
  secure                     1
  keyFile                    /path/to/your/privatekey.pem
  certFile                   /path/to/your/certificate.pem
}
```

Domain Name Configuration

Configuring domain names allows LiteSpeed to serve multiple websites from a single server.

```
virtualHost Example {
  vhRoot                     /var/www/example
  configFile
/usr/local/lsws/conf/vhosts/Example/vhconf.conf
  domainNames                example.com,www.example.com
}
```

Serving Static Assets

LiteSpeed can serve static assets efficiently by specifying the root directory of the website.

```
virtualHost Example {
  vhRoot                    /var/www/example
  docRoot                   /var/www/example/html
  configFile
/usr/local/lsws/conf/vhosts/Example/vhconf.conf
  domainNames               example.com,www.example.com
}
```

Command	Description
sudo /usr/local/lsws/bin/lswsctrl start	Start the LiteSpeed server.
sudo /usr/local/lsws/bin/lswsctrl stop	Stop the LiteSpeed server.
sudo /usr/local/lsws/bin/lswsctrl restart	Restart the LiteSpeed server.
sudo /usr/local/lsws/bin/lswsctrl reload	Reload the LiteSpeed server configuration.
sudo /usr/local/lsws/bin/lswsctrl status	Check the current status of the LiteSpeed server.
sudo /usr/local/lsws/bin/lswsctrl graceful	Perform a graceful restart of the LiteSpeed server.
sudo /usr/local/lsws/bin/lswsctrl configtest	Test the LiteSpeed server configuration for errors.
sudo /usr/local/lsws/bin/lswsctrl help	Display help information for LiteSpeed commands.

Database

MySQL

Command	Description
mysql -u <username> -p	Access MySQL from the terminal
mysql -u <username> -p <database>	Access a specific database directly from the terminal
mysqldump -u <username> -p <database> > db_backup.sql	Export a database dump to a SQL file
SHOW DATABASES;	Show all databases
CREATE DATABASE <database>;	Create a new database
DROP DATABASE <database>;	Delete a database
USE <database>;	Select and use a database
SELECT DATABASE();	Determine the current database in use
NOW();	MySQL function for the current date and time
SHOW TABLES;	Show all tables in the current database
DELETE FROM <table>;	Delete all records from a table
TRUNCATE TABLE <table>;	Delete all records from a table, but keep the table
DROP TABLE <table>;	Delete a table
DESCRIBE <table>;	Show the structure of a table
SHOW INDEX FROM <table>;	List all indexes on a table
CREATE TABLE <table> (<column-a> VARCHAR(120), <column-b> DATETIME);	Create a new table with specified columns
ALTER TABLE <table> ADD COLUMN <column> VARCHAR(120);	Add a new column to a table
ALTER TABLE <table> ADD COLUMN <column> int NOT NULL AUTO_INCREMENT PRIMARY KEY;	Add an auto-incrementing primary key column
INSERT INTO <table> (<column>, <column>) VALUES ('<value>', '<value>');	Insert a new record into a table
SELECT * FROM <table>;	Select all records from a table
SELECT <column>, <column> FROM <table>;	Select specific columns from a table
SELECT <table1>.<column>, <table1>.<another-column>, <table2>.<column> FROM <table1>, <table2>;	Select from multiple tables
SELECT COUNT(<column>) FROM <table>;	Count the number of records in a table
UPDATE <table> SET <column> = '<updated-value>' WHERE <column> = <value>;	Update specific records in a table
DELETE FROM <table> WHERE <column> = <value>;	Delete specific records from a table
SELECT User,Host FROM mysql.user;	List all MySQL users
CREATE USER 'username'@'localhost' IDENTIFIED BY 'password';	Create a new MySQL user
GRANT ALL ON <database>.* TO 'user'@'localhost';	Grant all privileges on a database to a user
1' OR '1'='1; -- `	SQL injection to bypass authentication
' OR 1=1; --	SQL injection to bypass login
1' AND 1=0 UNION SELECT null, version(); --	SQL injection to retrieve database version
1' UNION SELECT table_name, column_name FROM information_schema.columns WHERE table_schema=database(); --	SQL injection to list all tables and columns
' UNION SELECT username, password FROM users; --	SQL injection to dump user credentials

PostgreSQL

Command	Description
psql -U <username> -d <database> -h <hostname>	Connect to database
\q or \!	Disconnect from database
\copy <table_name> TO '<file_path>' CSV	Export database to csv
\l	Show all databases
CREATE DATABASE <database_name> WITH OWNER <username>;	Create new database
DROP DATABASE IF EXISTS <database_name>;	Delete database
\c <database_name>	Select and use database
SELECT current_database();	Determine what database is in use
current_timestamp	Postgres function for datetime input
\dt	Show all tables
DELETE FROM <table_name>;	Delete all records in a table
DROP TABLE IF EXISTS <table_name> CASCADE;	Delete table
\d+ <table name>	Show table structure
\d <table name>	List all indexes on a table
CREATE TABLE <table name>(<column> VARCHAR(216), <column> timestamp);	Create new table with columns of characters and datetime
ALTER TABLE <table_name> IF EXISTS ADD <column_name> <data_type> [<constraints>];	Add a column
ALTER TABLE <table_name> ADD COLUMN <column_name> SERIAL PRIMARY KEY;	Add a column with an unique, auto-incrementing ID

INSERT INTO <table_name> VALUES(<value_1>, <value_2>);	Insert a record
SELECT * FROM <table_name> WHERE <column_name> = <value>;	Select records
SELECT COUNT(*) FROM table_name WHERE condition;	Count records
UPDATE <table_name> SET <column_1> = <value_1>, <column_2> = <value_2> WHERE <column_1> = <value>;	Update records
DELETE FROM <table_name> WHERE <column_name> = <value>;	Delete records
\du	List all users
CREATE USER <user_name> WITH PASSWORD '<password>';	Create new user
GRANT ALL PRIVILEGES ON DATABASE <db_name> TO <user_name>;	Grant ALL access to user for * tables

MS SQL

Command	Description
sqlcmd -S localhost -U <user> -P '<password>'	Access MS SQL from the terminal
BACKUP DATABASE <database> TO DISK = '<file>';	Export a database dump
SELECT name FROM master..sysdatabases;	Show all databases
CREATE DATABASE <database-name>	Create a new database
DROP DATABASE <database-name>;	Delete a database
USE <database-name>;	Select and use a database
SELECT DB_NAME();	Determine the current database in use
SELECT getdate();	MS SQL function for current date and time
SELECT name FROM <database>..sysobjects WHERE xtype = 'U';	Show all tables in the database
DELETE FROM <table>;	Delete all records from a table
TRUNCATE TABLE <table>;	Delete all records in a table, but keep the table
DROP TABLE <table-name>;	Delete a table
SELECT * FROM INFORMATION_SCHEMA.COLUMNS WHERE TABLE_NAME='<table>';	Show table structure
EXEC sp_helpindex '[SCHEMA-NAME.<table>]';	List all indexes on a table
CREATE TABLE <table> (<column-name> varchar(255), <date> DATETIME);	Create a new table with specified columns
ALTER TABLE <table> ADD <column> <datatype>;	Add a new column to a table
ALTER TABLE <table> ADD <column> int IDENTITY(1,1) PRIMARY KEY;	Add an auto-incrementing primary key column
INSERT INTO <table> (<column>) VALUES ('<value>');	Insert a new record into a table
SELECT * FROM <table> WHERE <condition>;	Select records from a table
SELECT DISTINCT <column1>, <column2> FROM <table>;	Select distinct records from a table
SELECT COUNT(<column>) FROM <table> WHERE <condition>;	Count records that match a condition
SELECT COUNT(*) FROM <table>;	Count all records in a table
UPDATE <table> SET <column> = '<var>' WHERE <condition>;	Update specific records in a table
DELETE FROM <table> WHERE <condition>;	Delete specific records from a table
SELECT name FROM master..syslogins;	List all users
CREATE USER <user> WITH PASSWORD = '<password>';	Create a new user
GRANT ALL PRIVILEGES ON *.* TO <user>;	Grant all privileges to a user
1' OR '1'='1'; --	SQL injection to bypass authentication
1' AND 1=0 UNION SELECT null, @@version; –	SQL injection to retrieve database version
1' UNION SELECT table_name, column_name FROM information_schema.columns WHERE table_schema=DB_NAME(); –	SQL injection to list all tables and columns
1' UNION SELECT name, password_hash FROM sys.sql_logins; –	SQL injection to dump user credentials

Text Editors

VIM

VIM (Vi IMproved) is a highly configurable text editor built to enable efficient text editing. It is an enhanced version of the vi editor distributed with most UNIX systems. VIM is designed for use both from a command-line interface and as a standalone application in a graphical user interface. Its features include extensive support for programming languages, file formats, and integration with various tools, making it a popular choice among developers and system administrators.

Exiting VIM / Saving File

Command	Description
:qa	Close all files
:qa!	Close all files, abandon changes
:w	Save
:wq / :x	Save and close file
:q	Close file
:q!	Close file, abandon changes
ZZ	Save and quit
ZQ	Quit without checking changes

Navigation

Command	Description
h j k l	Arrow keys
<C-U> / <C-D>	Half-page up/down
<C-B> / <C-F>	Page up/down
Words	
b / w	Previous/next word
ge / e	Previous/next end of word
Line	
0 *(zero)*	Start of line

^	Start of line *(after whitespace)*
$	End of line
Character	
fc	Go forward to character c
Fc	Go backward to character c
Document	
gg	First line
G	Last line
:n	Go to line n
nG	Go to line n
Window	
zz	Center this line
zt	Top this line
zb	Bottom this line
H	Move to top of screen
M	Move to middle of screen
L	Move to bottom of screen
Search	
n	Next matching search pattern
N	Previous match
*	Next whole word under cursor
#	Previous whole word under cursor
Tab pages	
:tabedit [file]	Edit file in a new tab
:tabfind [file]	Open file if exists in new tab
:tabclose	Close current tab
:tabs	List all tabs
:tabfirst	Go to first tab
:tablast	Go to last tab

:tabn	Go to next tab
:tabp	Go to previous tab

Editing

Command	Description
a	Append
A	Append from end of line
i	Insert
o	Next line
O	Previous line
s	Delete char and insert
S	Delete line and insert
C	Delete until end of line and insert
r	Replace one character
R	Enter Replace mode
u	Undo changes
<C-R>	Redo changes
Esc / <C-[>	Exit insert mode
<C-C>	Exit insert mode, and abort current command

Copy / Paste

Command	Description
x	Delete character
dd	Delete line *(Cut)*
yy	Yank line *(Copy)*
p	Paste
P	Paste before
"*p / "+p	Paste from system clipboard
"*y / "+y	Paste to system clipboard

EMACS

Scrolling & Windows

Command	Description
CTRL-v	Scroll down (toward end of buffer)
M-v	Scroll up (toward beginning of buffer)
CTRL-M-v	Scroll other window down
CTRL-x 1	One window on current buffer
CTRL-x 2	Split window vertically
CTRL-x 3	Split window horizontally
CTRL-x ^	Grow window vertically; prefix is number of lines

File & Buffers

Command	Description
CTRLx CTRL-f	Find file (or create if not there); prompts for file name
CTRL-x CTRL-s	Save file
CTRLx CTRL-w	Write file; prompts for new name
CTRL-x s	Save modified buffers; asks about each
CTRL-x b	Select buffer; prompts for buffer name
CTRL-x CTRL-b	List buffers; shows in other window
CTRL-x k	Kill buffer; prompts for buffer name

Copy / Paste

Command	Description
CTRL-SPC	Mark one end of region
CTRL-w	Cut (after you Mark and move to other end)
M-w	Copy (after you Mark and move to other end)
CTRL-y	Yank (paste) most recently killed (cut or copied); will also use text currently selected in another application.
M-y	Next most recently killed (do C-y first, repeat M-y to cycle thru all)

Search & Replace

Command	Description
CTRL-s	Incremental search forward; searches as you type
CTRL-r	Incremental search backward
CTRL-M-s	Regexp search forward (there are differences in Emacs regexp syntax wrt Perl, etc.)
CTRL-M-r	Regexp search backward
M-x replace-string RET	String replace from here to end of buffer; prompts for string and replacement
M-x query-replace RET	String replace from here to end of buffer, querying for each occurrence
M-x grep RET	Prompts for a grep command, shows hits in a buffer
CTRL-x `	Visit next grep hit

Scripting

Python

Command	Result
arg=<value>	creates variable arg and assigns <value>
print(arg)	prints value of arg
del arg	removes variable arg
#comment	single line comment
/* <comment> */	multiple line comment
arr = []	initialize empty array
arr = ['A','B','C']	initialize array of strings
arr = [1,2,3]	initialize array of integers
arr[0]	access first index of array
arr[value]	access value index of array
arr = [i for i in range(1, 10)]	initialize array of integers with values 1 - 10
arr.append('<value>')	add <value> to array
user=input("Input value")	takes user input and assigns to variable user
dict = {}	initialize empty dictionary
dict = {'name1':1,'name2':2}	creates a dictionary
var == value	checks if var is equal to value
var != value	checks if var is not equal to value
var > value	checks if var is greater than value
var >= value	checks if var is greater than or equal to value
var < value	checks if var is less than value
var <= value	checks if var is less than or equal to value

Bash

Command	Result
arg=<value>	creates variable arg and assigns <value>
print(arg)	prints value of arg
del arg	removes variable arg
#comment	single line comment
/* <comment> */	multiple line comment
declare -a <array_name>	initialize empty array
arr=(A B C)	initialize array of strings
arr=(1 2 3)	initialize array of integers
echo ${arr[0]}	access first index of array
echo ${arr[X]}	access X index of array
arr+=(D E)	add new elements to the array
for i in ${arr[@]}	loop through array
read -p "Enter Value: " arg	takes user input and assigns to variable arg
dict=(["Name1"]="1" ["Name2"]="2")	create a dictionary
dict = {'name1':1,'name2':2}	creates a dictionary
var == value	checks if var is equal to value
var != value	checks if var is not equal to value
var > value	checks if var is greater than value
var >= value	checks if var is greater than or equal to value
var < value	checks if var is less than value
var <= value	checks if var is less than or equal to value
-z val	true if the string length is zero
-n val	true if the string length is non zero

Perl

Basic Syntax

($a, $b) = shift(@ARGV);	read command line params
sub p{my $var = shift; ...}	define subroutine
p(“bla”);	execute subroutine
if(expr){} elsif {} else {}	conditional
unless (expr){}	negative conditional
while (expr){}	while-loop
until (expr){}	until-loop
do {} until (expr)	postcheck until-loop
for($i=1; $i<=10; $i++){}	for-loop
foreach $i (@list){}	foreach-loop
last, next, redo	end loop, skip to next, jump to top
eval {$a=$a/$b; }; warn $@ if $@;	exception handling

Input/Output

<table>
<tr><td>open(INFILE,"in.txt") or die;</td><td>open file for input</td></tr>
<tr><td>open(INFILE,"<:utf8","file");</td><td>open file with encoding</td></tr>
<tr><td>open(TMP, "+>", undef);</td><td>open anonymous temp file</td></tr>
<tr><td>open(MEMORY,'>', \$var);</td><td>open in-memory-file</td></tr>
<tr><td>open(OUT,">out.txt") or die;</td><td>open output file</td></tr>
<tr><td>open(LOG,">>my.log") or die;</td><td>open file for append</td></tr>
<tr><td>open(PRC,"caesar <$file |");</td><td>read from process</td></tr>
<tr><td>open(EXTRACT, "|sort >Tmp$$");</td><td>write to process</td></tr>
<tr><td>$line = <INFILE>;</td><td>get next line</td></tr>
<tr><td>@lines = <INFILE>;</td><td>slurp infile</td></tr>
<tr><td>foreach $line (<STDIN>){...}</td><td>loop of lines from STDIN</td></tr>
<tr><td>print STDERR "Warning 1.\n";</td><td>print to STDERR</td></tr>
<tr><td>close INFILE;</td><td>close filehandle</td></tr>
</table>

Arrays and Lists

@a = (1..5);	array initialization

$i = @a;	number of elements in @a
($a, $b) = ($b, $a);	swap $a and $b
$x = $a[1];	access to index 1
$i = $#a;	last index in @a
push(@a, $s);	appends $s to @a
$a = pop(@a);	removes last element
chop(@a);	remove last char (per el.)
$a = shift(@a);	removes first element
reverse(@a);	reverse @a
@a = sort{$ela <=> $elb}(@a);	sort numerically
@a = split(/-/,$s);	split string into @a
$s = join(", " @c);	join @a elements into string
@a2 = @a[1,2,6..9];	array slice
@a2 = grep(!/^#/, @a);	remove comments from @a
Scalars and Strings	
chomp($str);	discard trailing \n
$v = chop($str);	$v becomes trailing char
eq, ne, lt, gt, le, ge, cmp	string comparison
$str = "0" x 4;	$str is now "0000"
$v = index($str, $x);	find index of $x in $str,
$v = rindex($str, $x);	starting from left or right
$v = substr($str, $strt, $len);	extract substring
$cnt = $sky =~ tr/0-9//;	count the digits in $sky
$str =~ tr/a-zA-Z/ /cs;	change non-alphas to space
$v = sprintf("%10s %08d",-$s,$n);	format string
Format String:	%[flags][0][width][.precision][mod]type
types	
c	character
d(i)	signed decimal int
e(E)	scientific notation
f	decimal floating point

g, G	shorter %e or %f / %E or %f
o	signed octal
s	string of chars
u, x, X	unsigned decimal int / hex int / hex int in caps
p	address pointer
n	nothing printed
modifiers: h,l,L	arg is short int / long int, double/ long double

Networking

Berkeley Packet Filter (BPF)

<table>
<tr><th colspan="2">BPF</th></tr>
<tr><th>Option</th><th>Description</th></tr>
<tr><td>[src|dst] host <host></td><td>Matches a host as the IP source, destination, or either</td></tr>
<tr><td>ether [src|dst] host <ehost></td><td>Matches a host as the Ethernet source, destination, or either</td></tr>
<tr><td>gateway host <host></td><td>Matches packets which used host as a gateway</td></tr>
<tr><td>[src|dst] net <network>/<len></td><td>Matches packets to or from an endpoint residing in network</td></tr>
<tr><td>[tcp|udp] [src|dst] port <port></td><td>Matches TCP or UDP packets sent to/from port</td></tr>
<tr><td>[tcp|udp] [src|dst] portrange <p1>-<p2></td><td>Matches TCP or UDP packets to/from a port in the given range</td></tr>
<tr><td>less <length></td><td>Matches packets less than or equal to length</td></tr>
<tr><td>greater <length></td><td>Matches packets greater than or equal to length</td></tr>
<tr><td>(ether|ip|ip6) proto <protocol></td><td>Matches an Ethernet, IPv4, or IPv6 protocol</td></tr>
<tr><td>(ether|ip) broadcast</td><td>Matches Ethernet or IPv4 broadcasts</td></tr>
<tr><td>(ether|ip|ip6) multicast</td><td>Matches Ethernet, IPv4, or IPv6 multicasts</td></tr>
<tr><td>type (mgt|ctl|data) [subtype <subtype>]</td><td>Matches 802.11 frames based on type and optional subtype</td></tr>
<tr><td>vlan [<vlan>]</td><td>Matches 802.1Q frames, optionally with a VLAN ID of vlan</td></tr>
<tr><td>mpls [<label>]</td><td>Matches MPLS packets, optionally with a label of label</td></tr>
<tr><td><expr> <relop> <expr></td><td>Matches packets by an arbitrary expression</td></tr>
</table>

TCP Flags
tcp-syn, tcp-ack, tcp-fin, tcp-psh, tcp-rst, tcp-urg
Protocols
tcp, udp, icmp, ip, ip6, wlan, arp, ether, link, tr, fddi, ppp, radio, rarp, slip

GIT

Init	
git init	initialize an existing directory as a Git repository
git clone <url>	retrieve an entire repository from a hosted location via URL
Stage	
git status	show modified files in working directory, staged for your next commit
git add <file>	add a file as it looks now to your next commit (stage)
git reset <file>	unstage a file while retaining the changes in working directory
git diff	diff of what is changed but not staged
git diff --staged	diff of what is staged but not yet committed
git commit -m "[descriptive message]"	commit your staged content as a new commit snapshot
Branch/Merge	
git branch	list your branches. a * will appear next to the currently active branch
git branch <branch-name>	create a new branch at the current commit
git checkout	switch to another branch and check it out into your working directory
git merge <branch>	merge the specified branch's history into the current one
git log	show all commits in the current branch's history
Share/Update	
git remote add <alias> <url>	add a git URL as an alias
git fetch <alias>	fetch down all the branches from that Git remote
git merge <alias>/<branch>	merge a remote branch into your current branch to bring it up to date
git push <alias> <branch>	Transmit local branch commits to the remote repository branch
git pull	fetch and merge any commits from the tracking remote branch

Docker

Docker is a powerful platform designed to simplify and accelerate the development, shipping, and deployment of applications. By leveraging containerization technology, Docker allows developers to package applications and their dependencies into a standardized unit called a container. These containers are lightweight, portable, and can run consistently across various computing environments, making Docker an essential tool for modern DevOps practices and microservices architectures. Key features of Docker include containerization, which encapsulates applications and their dependencies into containers ensuring consistent behavior across different environments, and portability, as containers can run on any system that supports Docker, including laptops, on-premises servers, and cloud platforms. Docker also provides isolation, enhancing security and reducing conflicts, and scalability, facilitating easy horizontal scaling of applications by deploying multiple container instances. Additionally, Docker ensures efficiency as containers are lightweight and share the host system's kernel, leading to better resource utilization compared to traditional virtual machines.

About Docker

Docker consists of several components that work together to provide a comprehensive containerization solution. At the core is the Docker Engine, which includes the Docker Daemon (`dockerd`), a background service responsible for managing containers, images, networks, and volumes, and the Docker CLI (`docker`), a command-line interface used to interact with the Docker daemon and perform various operations like building, running, and managing containers. Docker Images are immutable, read-only templates that contain the application code, runtime, libraries, and dependencies needed to run an application. These images are built using Dockerfiles, which define the steps to create the image. Docker Containers are instances of Docker images that are executable, running applications in isolated environments to ensure consistency across development, testing, and production stages.

Docker Hub is a cloud-based registry service that allows users to find, share, and publish Docker images, providing a vast repository of pre-built images for various applications and services. Docker Compose is a tool for defining and running multi-container Docker applications using a YAML file, simplifying the management of complex applications by allowing developers to define services, networks, and volumes in a single file. Docker Swarm is Docker's native clustering and orchestration tool, enabling users to manage a cluster of Docker engines as a single entity and providing features like load balancing, service discovery, and automated scaling. Docker Desktop is an application for Windows and macOS that offers an easy-to-use interface for managing Docker environments, including Docker Engine, Docker CLI, Docker Compose, and Kubernetes, making it ideal for local development.

Using Docker brings several benefits. It streamlines development by ensuring applications run the same way in development, testing, and production environments, thus reducing the "it works on my machine" problem. It facilitates rapid deployment as containers can be quickly started, stopped, and replicated, allowing for quick scaling of applications. Docker's resource efficiency, compared to traditional virtual machines, leads to better utilization of hardware and lower operational costs. The containerization model aligns well with microservices architecture, enabling developers to build, deploy, and manage discrete services independently. Moreover, Docker integrates seamlessly with various tools and platforms, including CI/CD pipelines, cloud services, and orchestration frameworks like Kubernetes. By leveraging Docker, organizations can achieve greater agility, efficiency, and reliability in their software development and deployment processes.

Command	Description
docker run -it <container> bash	Run a bash shell inside an image
docker ps -a	List all containers
docker stop <container>	Stop a container
docker rm <container>	Remove a stopped container
docker exec -it <container> bash	Execute and access bash inside a container
docker images	List the images
docker pull <image>	Pull an image or a repository from the registry
docker build -t <dockerfile>	Build the image from a Dockerfile
docker start <container>	Start a stopped container
docker restart <container>	Restart a running container
docker logs <container>	Fetch the logs of a container
docker inspect <container>	Return low-level information on a container
docker network ls	List all networks
docker network create <network>	Create a new network
docker network rm <network>	Remove a network
docker volume ls	List all volumes
docker volume create <volume>	Create a new volume
docker volume rm <volume>	Remove a volume
docker cp <container>:<path> <path>	Copy files/folders between a container and the local filesystem
docker commit <container> <image>	Create a new image from a container's changes
docker tag <image> <repository>	Tag an image to a repository
docker push <repository>	Push an image or a repository to the registry
docker-compose up	Create and start containers from a docker-compose file
docker-compose down	Stop and remove containers, networks, images, and volumes defined in a docker-compose file

Docker Compose

Docker Compose is a tool that simplifies the management of multi-container Docker applications. It allows developers to define and run applications using multiple containers through a single YAML file, known as a `docker-compose.yml`. This file specifies how the different services that make up the application should be configured and interconnected, enabling the entire application stack to be started with a single command. Docker Compose offers several key features: it allows for the definition of each service in the `docker-compose.yml` file, where each service corresponds to a container with various configurable options such as the image to use, environment variables, volumes to mount, ports to expose, and networks to connect to. With Docker Compose, you can use simple commands like `docker-compose up` to start all the defined services and `docker-compose down` to stop and remove them, greatly simplifying the process of managing multi-container applications. Docker Compose also enables environment isolation, allowing you to define and manage multiple isolated environments on a single host. It takes care of the orchestration of services, ensuring that dependencies are started in the correct order, and facilitates scaling services to handle increased load by specifying the number of container instances to run for a particular service.

Example docker-compose.yml:

```
version: '3'
services:
  web:
    image: my-web-app:latest
    ports:
      - "80:80"
    depends_on:
      - db
  db:
    image: mysql:5.7
    environment:
      MYSQL_ROOT_PASSWORD: example
    volumes:
      - db-data:/var/lib/mysql
volumes:
  db-data:
```

Dockerfiles

A Dockerfile is a script containing a series of instructions on how to build a Docker image. Each instruction in a Dockerfile creates a layer in the image, making it efficient to update and distribute images, as only the layers that have changed need to be rebuilt and redistributed. Dockerfiles provide a way to automate the process of creating custom Docker images, ensuring consistency and repeatability. Key instructions in a Dockerfile include `FROM` to specify the base image, `RUN` to execute commands and install software packages, `COPY` to copy files or directories from the local filesystem into the image, `ADD` to copy files from a URL or extract TAR files, `CMD` to provide the default command to run when a container is started, and `ENTRYPOINT` to configure a container to run as an executable. Other instructions include `ENV` to set environment variables, `EXPOSE` to inform Docker that the container listens on specified network ports at runtime, and `VOLUME` to create a mount point with the specified path and mark it as holding externally mounted volumes from the native host or other containers.

Example Dockerfile:

```
# Use an official Python runtime as a parent image
FROM python:3.8-slim

# Set the working directory in the container
WORKDIR /usr/src/app

# Copy the current directory contents into the container at
/usr/src/app
COPY . .

# Install any needed packages specified in requirements.txt
RUN pip install --no-cache-dir -r requirements.txt

# Make port 80 available to the world outside this container
EXPOSE 80

# Define environment variable
ENV NAME World

# Run app.py when the container launches
CMD ["python", "app.py"]
```

KubeCTL

Kubernetes is an open-source platform designed to automate the deployment, scaling, and management of containerized applications. It groups containers that make up an application into logical units for easy management and discovery. Kubernetes, often abbreviated as K8s, provides a robust environment to orchestrate containerized applications across a cluster of machines.

Concept	Description
Cluster	A set of nodes (physical or virtual machines) managed by Kubernetes.
Node	A worker machine in Kubernetes, part of the cluster.
Pod	The smallest and simplest Kubernetes object. Represents a single instance of a running process in a cluster.
Service	An abstraction which defines a logical set of Pods and a policy by which to access them.
Deployment	Provides declarative updates to applications and ensures the desired state.
ConfigMap	Provides configuration data to Pods.
Secret	Provides sensitive information like passwords to Pods.

Setting Up Kubernetes

To set up Kubernetes, you need a cluster of machines, either physical or virtual. Kubernetes supports various deployment methods, including using managed services such as Google Kubernetes Engine (GKE), Amazon EKS, or self-managed setups using tools like kubeadm, kops, or minikube for local development.

Prerequisites

- **Linux Environment**: Kubernetes nodes typically run on Linux distributions like Ubuntu or CentOS.
- **Docker**: Ensure Docker is installed and running on all nodes.
- **Kubectl**: The command-line tool for interacting with the Kubernetes cluster.

Create Resource

Command	Description
kubectl create namespace [namespace-name]	Create a new namespace
kubectl create -f [filename]	Create a resource from a JSON or YAML file

Kubectl Commands

Delete Resource

Command	Description
kubectl delete -f pod.yaml	Remove a pod using the name and type listed in pod.yaml
kubectl delete pods,services -l [label-key]=[label-value]	Remove all pods and services with a specific label
kubectl delete pods –all	Remove all pods (the command includes uninitialized pods as well)

List Resource

Command	Description
kubectl get namespaces	Generate a plain-text list of all namespaces
kubectl get pods	Generate a plain-text list of all pods
kubectl get pods -o wide	Generate a detailed plain-text list of all pods, containing information such as node name
kubectl get pods –field-selector=spec.nodeName=[server-name]	Generate a list of all pods running on a particular node server
kubectl get replicationcontroller [replication-controller-name]	List a specific replication controller in plain-text
kubectl get replicationcontroller,services	Generate a plain-text list of all replication controllers and services
kubectl get daemonset	Generate a plain-text list of all daemon sets

Update a Resource

Command	Description
kubectl apply -f [service-name].yaml	Create a new service with the definition contained in [service-name].yaml
kubectl apply -f [controller-name].yaml	Create a new replication controller with the definition contained in [controller-name].yaml
kubectl apply -f [directory-name]	Create the objects defined in any .yaml, .yml, or .json file in a directory
kubectl edit svc/[service-name]	Update a resource by editing it in a text editor

Resource State

Command	Description
kubectl describe nodes [node-name]	View details about a particular node
kubectl describe pods [pod-name]	View details about a particular pod
kubectl describe -f pod.json	Display details about a pod whose name and type are listed in pod.json
kubectl describe pods [replication-controller-name]	See details about all pods managed by a specific replication controller
kubectl describe pods	Show details about all pods

Executing Commands

Command	Description
kubectl exec [pod-name] -- [command]	Receive output from a command run on the first container in a pod
kubectl exec [pod-name] -c [container-name] – [command]	Get output from a command run on a specific container in a pod
kubectl exec -ti [pod-name] -- /bin/bash	Run /bin/bash from a specific pod. The received output comes from the first container

Modifying kubeconfig

Command	Description
kubectl config current-context	Display the current context
kubectl config set-cluster [cluster-name] --server=[server-name]	Set a cluster entry in kubeconfig
kubectl config unset [property-name]	Unset an entry in kubeconfig

Print Logs

Command	Description
kubectl logs [pod-name]	Syntax for printing logs
kubectl logs -f [pod-name]	Stream logs from a pod

Common kubectl have short names as some of the full long names get to be difficult to work with.

Short Name	Long Name
csr	certificatesigningrequests
cs	componentstatuses
cm	configmaps
ds	daemonsets
deploy	deployments
ep	endpoints
ev	events
hpa	horizontalpodautoscalers
ing	ingresses
limits	limitranges
ns	namespaces
no	nodes
pvc	persistentvolumeclaims
pv	persistentvolumes
po	pods
pdb	poddisruptionbudgets
psp	podsecuritypolicies
rs	replicasets
rc	replicationcontrollers
quota	resourcequotas
sa	serviceaccounts
svc	services

MISC

User Agents

Browser/Device	User Agent
Google Chrome	Mozilla/5.0 (Windows NT 10.0; Win64; x64) AppleWebKit/537.36 (KHTML, like Gecko) Chrome/112.0.5615.138 Safari/537.36
Mozilla Firefox	Mozilla/5.0 (Windows NT 10.0; Win64; x64; rv:102.0) Gecko/20100101 Firefox/102.0
Microsoft Edge	Mozilla/5.0 (Windows NT 10.0; Win64; x64) AppleWebKit/537.36 (KHTML, like Gecko) Chrome/112.0.5615.138 Safari/537.36 Edge/112.0.1722.64
Apple Safari	Mozilla/5.0 (Macintosh; Intel Mac OS X 10_15_7) AppleWebKit/605.1.15 (KHTML, like Gecko) Version/15.0 Safari/605.1.15
Microsoft Internet Explorer 11	Mozilla/5.0 (Windows NT 10.0; Win64; x64; Trident/7.0; rv:11.0) like Gecko
Apple iPad	Mozilla/5.0 (iPad; CPU OS 14_6 like Mac OS X) AppleWebKit/605.1.15 (KHTML, like Gecko) Version/14.0 Mobile/15E148 Safari/604.1
Apple iPhone	Mozilla/5.0 (iPhone; CPU iPhone OS 15_2 like Mac OS X) AppleWebKit/605.1.15 (KHTML, like Gecko) Version/15.0 Mobile/15E148 Safari/604.1
Googlebot	Mozilla/5.0 (compatible; Googlebot/2.1; +http://www.google.com/bot.html)
Bing Bot	Mozilla/5.0 (compatible; bingbot/2.0; +http://www.bing.com/bingbot.htm)
Samsung Phone	Mozilla/5.0 (Linux; Android 11; SAMSUNG SM-G998U Build/RP1A.200720.012) AppleWebKit/537.36 (KHTML, like Gecko) Chrome/92.0.4515.159 Mobile Safari/537.36
Samsung Galaxy Note 20	Mozilla/5.0 (Linux; Android 11; SAMSUNG SM-N986U Build/RP1A.200720.012) AppleWebKit/537.36 (KHTML, like Gecko) Chrome/92.0.4515.159 Mobile Safari/537.36
Google Pixel 6	Mozilla/5.0 (Linux; Android 12; Pixel 6 Build/SQ1D.211205.016.A4) AppleWebKit/537.36 (KHTML, like Gecko) Chrome/93.0.4577.62 Mobile Safari/537.36
HTC	Mozilla/5.0 (Linux; Android 9; HTC One M8 Build/PKQ1.180904.001) AppleWebKit/537.36 (KHTML, like Gecko) Chrome/92.0.4515.159 Mobile Safari/537.36
Curl	curl/7.79.1
Wget	Wget/1.21.2 (linux-gnu)
Lynx	Lynx/2.8.9rel.1 libwww-FM/2.14 SSL-MM/1.4.1 OpenSSL/1.1.1

Common Ports

Port	Service/Proto	Port	Service/Proto	Port	Service/Proto
7	echo	465	SMTP SSL	1589	CISCO VQP
20	ftp-data	512	rexec	1701	L2TP
21	ftp	513	rlogin	1723	PPTP
22	ssh	514	syslog	1741	CISCOWorks 2000
23	telnet	515	Line Printer Daemon	1755	Microsoft Media
25	smtp	520	RIP	1812-1813	RADIUS
42	name	521	RIPng	1863	MSN
43	nickname	522	ULP	2082-2083	cPanel
49	TACACS	524	NCP	2967	Symantec AV
53	DNS	530	RPC	3128	HTTP Proxy
67	bootps	540	UUCP	3260	iSCSI target
68	bootpc	554	RTSP	3306	MySQL
69	tftp	546-547	DHCPv6	3389	MS RDP
70	gopher	560	Remote Replication	3689	iTunes
79	finger	563	NNTPS	3690	Subversion
80	HTTP	587	SMTP Submission	4333	mSQL
88	kerberos	593	Microsoft DCOM	4664	Google Desktop
102	MS Exchange	631	Internet Printing	4899	radmin
110	POP3	636	LDAP SSL	5000	UPnP
113	ident	646	LDS	5001	iperf
119	NNTP	691	MS Exchange	5432	PostgreSQL
123	NTP	860	ISCI	5500	VNC Server
135	Microsoft RPC	873	rsync	6000-6001	X11
137-139	NetBIOS	902	VMware Server	6665-6669	IRC
143	IMAP4	989-990	FTP SSL	6679, 6697	IRC SSL
161-162	SNMP	993	IMAP4 SSL	8000	Internet Radio
177	XDMCP	995	POP3 SSL	8080	HTTP Proxy
179	BGP	1025	Microsoft RPC	8086-8087	Kaspersky AV
201	Appletalk	1026-1029	Microsoft Messenger	8200	VMware Server
264	BGMP	1080	Socks Proxy	9100	HP JetDirect
318	TSP	1194	OpenVPN	9800	WebDAV
389	LDAP	1241	Nessus	9090	Websphere
443	HTTPS	1311	Dell Open Manage	10000	Webmin
445	Microsoft DS	1433-1434	Microsoft SQL	11211	Memcached
464	Kerberos	1512	WINS	27017	MongoDB

IPV4

IPv4 Header

IPv4 Header					
	0		1	2	3
0	IP Version	Header Length	TOS	Total Length	
4	IP Identification			X D M	
8	TTL		Protocol	Checksum	
12	Source Address				
16	Destination Address				
20	Optional Options				

IPv4 ICMP Header

IPv4 ICMP Header				
	0	1	2	3
0	Type	Code	Checksum	
4	Optional Additional Information			

IPv4 Subnet Class Ranges

Class Address Ranges	
Class A	1.0.0.0 - 126.0.0.0
Class B	128.0.0.0 - 191.255.0.0
Class C	192.0.1.0 - 223.255.255.0

Reserved Addresses
10.0.0.0 -> 10.255.255.255
172.16.0.0 -> 172.31.255.255
192.168.0.0 -> 192.168.255.255
27.0.0.0 is reserved for loopback and IPC on the local host
224.0.0.0 -> 239.255.255.255 is reserved for multicast addresses

IPv4 Subnets

Network Bits	Subnet Mask	Number of Subnets	Number of Hosts
/8	255.0.0.0	0	16777214
/9	255.128.0.0	2 (0)	8388606
/10	255.192.0.0	4 (2)	4194302
/11	255.224.0.0	8 (6)	2097150
/12	255.240.0.0	16 (14)	1048574
/13	255.248.0.0	32 (30)	524286
/14	255.252.0.0	64 (62)	262142
/15	255.254.0.0	128 (126)	131070
/16	255.255.0.0	256 (254)	65534
/17	255.255.128.0	512 (510)	32766
/18	255.255.192.0	1024 (1022)	16382
/19	255.255.224.0	2048 (2046)	8190
/20	255.255.240.0	4096 (4094)	4094
/21	255.255.248.0	8192 (8190)	2046
/22	255.255.252.0	16384 (16382)	1022
/23	255.255.254.0	32768 (32766)	510
/24	255.255.255.0	65536 (65534)	254
/25	255.255.255.128	131072 (131070)	126
/26	255.255.255.192	262144 (262142)	62
/27	255.255.255.224	524288 (524286)	30
/28	255.255.255.240	1048576 (1048574)	14
/29	255.255.255.248	2097152 (2097150)	6
/30	255.255.255.252	4194304 (4194302)	2

Network Bits	Subnet Mask	Number of Subnets	Number of Hosts
/16	255.255.0.0	256 (254)	65534
/17	255.255.128.0	512 (510)	32766
/18	255.255.192.0	1024 (1022)	16382
/19	255.255.224.0	2048 (2046)	8190
/20	255.255.240.0	4096 (4094)	4094
/21	255.255.248.0	8192 (8190)	2046
/22	255.255.252.0	16384 (16382)	1022
/23	255.255.254.0	32768 (32766)	510
/24	255.255.255.0	65536 (65534)	254
/25	255.255.255.128	131072 (131070)	126
/26	255.255.255.192	262144 (262142)	62
/27	255.255.255.224	524288 (524286)	30
/28	255.255.255.240	1048576 (1048574)	14
/29	255.255.255.248	2097152 (2097150)	6
/30	255.255.255.252	4194304 (4194302)	2

Network Bits	Subnet Mask	Number of Subnets	Number of Hosts
/8	255.0.0.0	0	16777214
/9	255.128.0.0	2 (0)	8388606
/10	255.192.0.0	4 (2)	4194302
/11	255.224.0.0	8 (6)	2097150
/12	255.240.0.0	16 (14)	1048574
/13	255.248.0.0	32 (30)	524286
/14	255.252.0.0	64 (62)	262142
/15	255.254.0.0	128 (126)	131070

ICMPv4 Type Codes

Type	Code	Description
0	0	Echo Reply
3	0	Net Unreachable
	1	Host Unreachable
	2	Protocol Unreachable
	3	Port Unreachable
	4	Fragmentation Needed
	5	Source Route Failed
	6	Destination Network Unknown
	7	Destination Host Unknown
	8	Source Host Isolated
	9	Net Administratively Prohibited
	10	Host Administratively Prohibited
	11	Dest Net Unreachable for TOS
	12	Dest Host Unreachable for TOS
	13	Communication Administratively Prohibited
	14	Host Precedence Violation
	15	Precedence cutoff in effect
4	. 0	Source Quench (Deprecated)
5	0	Redirect Datagram for the Network
	1	Redirect Datagram for the Host
	2	Redirect Datagram for the TOS and Network
	3	Redirect Datagram for the TOS and Host
8	0	Echo
9	0	Normal router advertisement
	16	Does not route common traffic
11	0	Time to Live exceeded in Transit
	1	Fragment Reassembly Time Exceeded
12	0	Pointer indicates the error
	1	Missing a Required Option
	2	Bad Length
13	0	Timestamp
14	0	Timestamp Reply
15	0	Information Request (Deprecated)
16	0	Information Reply (Deprecated)
17	0	Address Mask Request (Deprecated)
18	0	Address Mask Reply (Deprecated)
30	0	Traceroute (Deprecated)

IPv6

IPv6 Header

IPv6 Header				
	0	1	2	3
0	Version	Traffic Class	Flow Label	
4	Payload Length		Next Header	Hop Limit
8	Source IP Network			
12	Source IP Network			
16	Source IP Interface			
20	Source IP Interface			
24	Destination IP Network			
28	Destination IP Network			
32	Destination IP Interface			
36	Destination IP Interface			

IPv6 ICMP Header

IPv6 ICMP Header				
	0	1	2	3
0	Type	Code	Checksum	
4	Optional Additional Information			

ICMPv6 Type Code

Type	Code	Description
0	0	Reserved
1	0	No Route to Destination
	1	Administrativly Prohibited
	2	Beyond Scope of Source Address
	3	Address Unreachable
	4	Port Unreachable
	5	Source Address Failed Ingress/Egress Policy
	6	Reject Route to Destination
	7	Error in Source Routing Header
2	0	Packet Too Big
3	0	hop limit exceeded in transit
	1	fragment reassembly time exceeded
4	0	erroneous header field encountered
	1	unrecognized Next Header type encountered
	2	unrecognized IPv6 option encountered
	3	IPv6 First Fragment has incomplete IPv6 Header Chain
	4	Precedence cutoff in effect
128	0	Echo Request
129	0	Echo Reply
130	0	Multicast Listener Query
131	0	Multicast Listener Report
132	0	Multicast Listener Done
133	0	Router Solicitation
134	0.	Router Advertisement
135	0	Neighbor Solicitation
136	0	Neighbor Advertisement
137	0	Redirect Message

TCP Header

TCP Header				
	0	1	2	3
0	Source Port		Destination Port	
4	Sequence Number			
8	Acknowledgment Number			
12	Source Address			
16	HL / R	Flags	Window Size	
20	Optional Options			

UDP Header

UDP Header				
	0	1	2	3
0	Source Port		Destination Port	
4	Length		Checksum	

DNS Header

DNS Header				
	0	1	2	3
0	Query ID		QR / Opcode / AA / TC / RD	RA / Z / AD / CD / Rcode
4	Query Count		Answer Count	
8	Total Authority Resource Records		Total Additional Resource Records	
12	DNS Data			

Legend

QR - Query[0] or Response[1], Opcode - Query[0], Inverse Query[1], Status[2], Notify[4], Update[5], AA - Authoritative Answer, TC - Truncated Response, RD - Recursion Desired, RA - Recursion Available, Z - Zero, AD - Authentic Data (DNSSEC), CD - Checking Disabled (DNSSEC), RCode - No Error[0], Format Error[1], Server Failure[2], Nonexistent domain[3], Query Type[4], Query Refused[5]

ARP Header

ARP Header				
	0	1	2	3
0	Hardware Address Type		Protocol Address Type	
4	HW Address Length	Protocol Address Length	OPCODE	
8	Source Hardware Address			
12	Source Hardware Address		Source Protocol Address	
16	Source Protocol Address		Target Hardware Address	
20	Target Hardware Address			
24	Target Protocol Address			

TTL and Windows Size by OS

Operating System	Time To Live	TCP Window Size
Linux (Kernel 2.4 and 2.6)	64	5840
Google Linux		5720
FreeBSD		65535
Windows XP	128	
Windows Vista +		8192
Cisco iOS 12.4	255	4128

Common Wireshark Filters

Filter	Description
eth.addr == XX:XX:XX:XX:XX:XX	Filter by mac address
eth.src == XX:XX:XX:XX:XX:XX	Filter by source mac address
eth.dst == XX:XX:XX:XX:XX:XX	Filter by destination mac address
eth.vlan.id = XX	Filter by VLAN id
ip.addr == X.X.X.X	Filter by IP X.X.X.X
ip.src == X.X.X.X	Filter by source IP X.X.X.X
ip.dst == X.X.X.X	Filter by destination IP X.X.X.X
tcp.port = XX	Filter by TCP port XX
tcp.srcport = XX	Filter by TCP source port XX
tcp.dstport = XX	Filter by TCP destination port XX
udp.port = XX	Filter by UDP port XX
udp.srcport = XX	Filter by UDP source port XX
udp.dstport = XX	Filter by UDP destination port XX
http	Filter HTTP traffic
dns	Filter DNS traffic
http.user_agent contains <browser>	Filter by User Agent browser string
!(arp or icmp or dns)	Filter out arp, icmp and dns traffic
tcp stream <number>	Filter by TCP stream

ASCII Table

ASCII	Hex	Char	ASCII	Hex	Char	ASCII	Hex	Char	ASCII	Hex	Char
0	0	NUL	28	1C	FS	56	38	8	88	58	X
1	1	SOH	29	1D	GS	57	39	9	89	59	Y
2	2	STX	30	1E	RS	58	3A	:	90	5A	Z
3	3	ETX	31	1F	US	59	3B	;	91	5B	[
4	4	EOT	32	20	(space)	60	3C	<	96	60	`
5	5	ENQ	33	21	!	61	3D	=	97	61	a
6	6	ACK	34	22	"	62	3E	>	98	62	b
7	7	BEL	35	23	#	63	3F	?	99	63	c
8	8	BS	36	24	$	64	40	@	100	64	d
9	9	TAB	37	25	%	65	41	A	101	65	e
10	A	LF	38	26	&	66	42	B	102	66	f
11	B	VT	39	27	'	67	43	C	103	67	g
12	C	FF	40	28	(	68	44	D	104	68	h
13	D	CR	41	29	)	69	45	E	105	69	i
14	E	SO	42	2A	*	70	46	F	106	6A	j
15	F	SI	43	2B	+	71	47	G	107	6B	k
16	10	DLE	44	2C	,	72	48	H	112	70	p
17	11	DC1	45	2D	-	73	49	I	113	71	q
18	12	DC2	46	2E	.	74	4A	J	114	72	r
19	13	DC3	47	2F	/	75	4B	K	115	73	s
20	14	DC4	48	30	0	80	50	P	116	74	t
21	15	NAK	49	31	1	81	51	Q	117	75	u
22	16	SYN	50	32	2	82	52	R	118	76	v
23	17	ETB	51	33	3	83	53	S	119	77	w
24	18	CAN	52	34	4	84	54	T	120	78	x
25	19	EM	53	35	5	85	55	U	121	79	y
26	1A	SUB	54	36	6	86	56	V	122	7A	z
27	1B	ESC	55	37	7	87	57	W	123	7B	{

Made in the USA
Monee, IL
09 October 2026

65323075R00085